Transparent Investing

How to Play the Stock Market without Getting Played

(A Data-Proven, Simple Investing Strategy)

PATRICK GEDDES

Copyright © 2021 by Patrick Geddes

All rights reserved. No part of this publication may be reproduced, distributed, or transmitted in any form or by any means, including photocopying, recording, or other electronic or mechanical methods, without the prior written permission of the publisher, except in the case of brief quotations embodied in critical reviews and certain other noncommercial uses permitted by copyright law.

Paperback ISBN: 979-8-9850064-0-7
Hardback ISBN: 979-8-9850064-1-4
E-book ISBN: 979-8-9850064-2-1

Manufactured and printed in the United States of America

Transparent Investing

Contents

To my late parents, Virginia and Francis,
who planted all the seeds from which this book sprang to life

Preface

IN 2006, *San Francisco Magazine* published an article on the history of indexing as an investment strategy. The article, "The Best Investment Advice You'll Never Get," quoted me and the other cofounder of the investment firm Aperio Group. Its publication resulted in more than seven hundred phone calls from investors seeking our services since the integrity of our "transparent investing" approach had been described so positively in the article.

One caller said, "I always suspected I was getting played by the investment industry, but after that article, I now understand how." She and many others were drawn to our firm's somewhat contrarian philosophy and approach to managing our clients' investments.

Even though our business wasn't focused on those types of clients, we saw a need and wanted to help. So we ran a couple of free seminars describing transparent investing. In 2007, I took the material from those seminars and created a free website, so any investor could access it. Thousands did. That content, updated, formed the beginnings of the book you now hold in your hands.

I felt driven to write this book for a couple of different reasons. First, I've been blessed with good fortune in the financial success of Aperio Group. On the one hand, I much enjoyed the analytic side of investing as an intellectual challenge, but I knew I couldn't work in a place where I'd have to lie (as defined by my rigid and prickly standards). That meant I could pretty much work only at a firm I had helped define, specifically to reflect our firm's name, since the Latin verb *aperio* means, "To make clear, reveal the truth." Then when Aperio Group grew to over a hundred employees and $42 billion in assets under management, I found I was the beneficiary of some unforeseen good luck.

I feel I have an obligation to try to repay somehow a world that had been so generous to me. This book is intended to help consumers feel more empowered as they face their own biases and interact with a biased industry, but to be honest, it also serves a somewhat selfish purpose for me as I try to rebalance the scales a little.

My second motivation comes from that fixation on the truth, as something I consider to be a sacred thing. When I observe any dishonesty, I get bothered, but when I know an industry and field as well as I know investing, it drives me to distraction to see consumers get fed a lot of self-serving garbage mixed in with the valid services from advisors that provide value.

The best way I know to improve things is to get consumers to vote with their dollars, as they have from 2010 to 2020, when so much in assets flowed out of active management and into indexing. I was overjoyed (and pleasantly surprised) to see consumers wising up about active management and putting such pressure on fees. The more consumers force their own interests first, ahead of the industry's profits, the better off all future consumers will be.

I envision Transparent Investing as a movement of enlightened consumers. The book, for me, is just a mechanism to make concrete all the issues, but the real goal is to change consumer behavior *for the benefit of consumers*, not for the benefit of those of us professionals in the investment field. This consumer advocacy drove this book as much as anything, and I sincerely hope that it helps you. If you find this book a benefit, please encourage the movement by telling others about it. And don't forget to check out patrickgeddes.co/transparent-investing, which is full of free resources and tools for investors and to which I will be periodically adding new content, courses, and more.

Introduction

IN MY EXPERIENCE, many investors seek the Holy Grail: the magic formula that will make them a killing in the market. They buy book after book, attend webinars, and even change advisors in hopes of discovering the secret they're sure exists.

Spoiler Alert: If you hope to find that kind of magic in this book, not only will I disappoint you by failing to provide those carefully guarded magic formulas but I'll also sound like a real wet blanket by declaring that the magic doesn't actually exist. That's right, Virginia. I'm afraid there is no Santa Claus after all.

Let's cut right to the chase with the three steps that *will* make you successful as an investor:

1. Determining what best fits your situation (how much of your portfolio should be in risky assets like stocks

or real estate and how much in safer assets like bonds or cash).

2. Investing in a few indexed strategies to match that allocation.
3. Not doing anything—adjusting your allocation or making withdrawals—until you need the money.

Aren't you thrilled you've finally learned the magic formula to amassing vast riches? No, of course not. Instead, you're probably wondering, "Do I really need an entire book to explain something this pathetically simple?"

Yes, in fact, we all do, because there's a catch: your brain is wired to think investing has to be more complicated.

Unfortunately for us all, our brains have evolved in ways that tend to make us poor investors. We make bad decisions about money not because we're stupid, but because, as the data show, we're anything *but* rational when it comes to investing. In fact, given the high emotional charge that finance carries for most of us in Western culture, money is a subject about which we're mostly *irrational*.

This is why part 1 of this book focuses on how your mind works with regard to investing. We'll see how the human brain has evolved over millions of years in ways that have been great for technological innovation and human achievement but not always ideal for investment decisions. By understanding the intricacies of how you operate when it comes to investing, you'll be empowered to achieve your financial goals more easily.

The counterintuitive philosophy of transparent investing—the core of which is laid out in the three steps above—is the culmination of my decades-long career as a leader of a high-level investment-management company (including watching how delightfully irrational we humans tend to be), and my passion for studying the academic research on indexing.

I cofounded the investment firm Aperio Group—a leader in something called customized indexing—in 1999, serving as Chief Investment Officer (CIO) and then Chief Executive Officer (CEO). We grew the firm to $42 billion in assets under management by the end of 2020, all without any funding. I served as Morningstar's first research director and helped build their research function in the 1990s, later becoming the firm's first Chief Financial Officer (CFO). I also spent five years as a corporate financial analyst for a large oil company. For many years, I taught graduate-level portfolio theory and advanced corporate finance, and I've had a number of investment articles published in fancy academically oriented journals. Last but not least, I have an MBA from one of the world's leading academic centers for investment research, the University of Chicago.

All that impressive experience means you should rely on my insights and advice about investing, right? Well, while these credentials may prove my expertise, they don't speak to my ethics and motivation, which comprise a big part of whether you should trust my advice.

Why do the ethics of investment advice matter so much? Because the investment industry has evolved to encourage some of *your* worst instincts because it makes *us* more money. While the investment industry measures success based on how well *we* do as investment managers, I believe our success should be measured by how well we do for *you*, the live people with actual portfolios.

That's why, in part 2, I'll provide the proof—in the form of published research—for how bad we professionals are at predicting two things: one, when the stock market will go up or down (called *market timing*), and two, which professional stock-pickers (defined as *active management*) will beat the market whether it's up or down. I'll explain how the investment industry blends helpful advice with self-serving recommendations, and I'll give you the insights you'll need to distinguish useful services from unreliable promises and focus on *your* success, not ours.

Then, in the final section of the book, part 3, I'll shift to the practical investment choices available, describing a now widely used approach to investing called indexing, or passive investing. These chapters provide important details about how to do indexing well and guide you through the critical choice of whether to hire a wealth advisor to manage your portfolio.

This book is about a kind of magic—just not the magic formula that will supposedly make you rich. Instead, it's about the magic that happens in your life when you become aware of how Homo sapiens think and behave and what you can control and what you can't, especially when it comes to investing.

To get the most out of our time together, please open yourself to a different approach to investing that may not square with your previous assumptions and beliefs. My hope is that, by the end of our journey, you'll feel empowered to create a brighter financial future for yourself by practicing transparent investing.

How Is This Book Different?

THIS BOOK'S PHILOSOPHIES OVERLAP with some other books on index investing, especially those by the late John Bogle, a particular hero of mine for his efforts to get investors to recognize how important fees are and how untrustworthy the investment industry can be (his devoted followers are called *Bogleheads*).

So what's different about *Transparent Investing*? For starters, a heavy emphasis on psychology and a little taste of philosophical wisdom. While other books may describe our foibles and biases as human beings, I also show you how to avoid the specific investment mistakes and pitfalls those foibles and biases can cause.

Another major difference is that *Transparent Investing* is one of the few investment books that objectively counsel on whether to hire a wealth advisor or how to identify the better ones if you do seek professional guidance. It's true: the science and art of picking investments is sexier than the nuts and bolts of hiring a financial professional. However, the latter may prove more important, as we'll see on the following pages.

You'll be a much better consumer if you understand how the industry really works, from its psychological biases to its methods for getting paid to its awful historical track record for making predictions. Slogging through the complexities of how fees get paid sounds like pretty dry stuff, but it's where analysis and math actually pay off (maybe more than your previous investments have!).

Yet another major difference between this book and other investment guides you may have read comes from a focus on humility, which means learning to avoid the temptation of sexy strategies that so appeal to our brains' wiring. While other books also stand for consumer advocacy, this one will provide a brutally honest look at the investment industry while teaching you how the game gets played and how to better assess credibility.

Giving up on some of the sizzle may prove hard, as it's so much more satisfying to think of ourselves as cleverly manipulating the world around us to our own financial benefit. Still, the numbers don't lie: research shows that *not* trying so hard will, on average, lead to a bigger portfolio, as counterintuitive as that may sound. And helping you get to a bigger portfolio is the most important job of any investment manager, regardless of how glamorous the path taken to get there.

How I Became a Self-Righteous and Irritating Evangelist

I GREW UP IN A HOUSEHOLD that valued pushing back. My parents displayed rebellious tendencies even as they both attended divinity school, where they met. During the 1960s, my father participated in the civil rights movement, getting arrested with the Freedom Riders in Mississippi in 1961, rebuilding a Black church burned down by white supremacists in 1964, and marching with Martin Luther King, Jr. in Selma in 1965. My father would observe the same provocative tendencies in his children and say that we, too, were "dung disturbers," although he used more colorful language.

Add to that rebellious streak an outrage when I watched those in power, like managers at companies where I worked early in my career, try to evade the truth when it served their own ends. I felt very much like the child in the Hans Christian

Andersen fairy tale "The Emperor's New Clothes"—the only one willing to say out loud, "But he hasn't got anything on!"

My youthful bafflement at how people in power could talk such claptrap (OK, I'll cop now to a certain naïveté throughout my life) led me to explore how the human mind operates. The first external source that caught my attention, around 2000, was a book about evolutionary psychology, *The Moral Animal*, by Robert Wright. The author discusses the scientific origin of self-deception and how humans developed a sensitivity to hypocrisy *in* others as well as the trait of signaling integrity (whether or not they have integrity) *to* others.

While *The Moral Animal* got me excited, the biggest influence on my thoughts about how we humans operate came from another book I read several years later, *The Happiness Hypothesis* by Jonathan Haidt. Like Wright, Haidt argues that humans developed self-deception partly as a survival skill, but he takes the idea even further in his analysis of brain function. He suggests that the primary job of the neocortex (the part of the brain that became enlarged more recently) is to come up with rationalizations that validate whatever the subconscious or emotional parts of the mind crave. In other words, the most rational part of our brain not only fails at times to offset the less rational elements of our psychology but actually conspires to *support* the irrational, proving who's really in the driver's seat.

I found Haidt's concepts both exciting and upsetting, and

I began looking around me in both my personal and professional lives. I found that I didn't just see *occasional* evidence of people making up reasons to justify whatever they wanted—I saw it all the time. It was depressing learning that humans are self-deceiving little beasts. Even more disturbing was looking in the mirror and observing that I, too, behaved that way, not just from time to time, but constantly.

A silver lining existed in all this insight though. It proved that I could develop my skill at spotting self-serving behavior and identify it more easily over time, hopefully even when it originated from me. Of course, the better I got at spotting that behavior, the more I needed to guard against getting too high and mighty (a tendency that comes unfortunately easily to many of us in the financial world). As we'll learn in parts 1 and 2 of this book, spotting your own and others' tendencies toward self-deception will prove an important skill in making wise investment choices.

I further refined these ideas after finding an author with a more practical approach. Annie Duke, a professional gambler, argues effectively in *Thinking in Bets* that the key to better decisions lies in thinking about the vast majority of life's challenges as more like poker (a game of some skill but a lot of chance) than like chess (a game relying almost entirely on skill). She emphasizes not only how important thinking in probabilities is but also how dangerous the mind's rationalizations are to good decision-making.

Thus, Transparent Investing, the philosophy, and *Transparent Investing*, the book, both evolved out of a weird mix of professional experience, rebelliousness, irritatingly high-minded moral outrage, and a lot of study. Watching how dishonest the investment industry can be about its predictive abilities truly enrages me. I want to shout at consumers, "Wake up and smell the coffee!" This book strives to be a coherent expression of that anger. I hope it helps you tell the difference between the services we investment managers provide that actually benefit you and the ones that benefit us at your expense.

Part I

YOUR BRAIN IS HAZARDOUS TO YOUR WEALTH

Chapter 1

Emotions Count More Than Math

A COUPLE OF YEARS AGO, I was chatting with a sophisticated wealth manager whose investment savvy and ethics I've admired for years. As she reflected on her twenty-plus years of experience working in the investment industry, she said, "You know, the longer I'm in this business, the more I realize that when working with investors, it's about 80 percent emotions and 20 percent math and analysis."

She went on to say that, for all her fine talk about quantitative analysis, clients' emotions remain the more important driver, in spite of how counterintuitive that might be. She didn't mean this as a complaint or evidence of foolishness, but rather as an accurate assessment of how investors, whether neophyte or expert, make choices that affect their financial future. I was struck by how this mirrored my own experiences in the financial sector.

However, this doesn't mean the quantitative analytic approach to investing is no longer relevant. I've spent forty years living in that world, and I have as much fun as the next "quant" throwing around terms like covariance matrix or leptokurtic logarithmic distributions when talking about investing. The problem arises when the emotional side of things gets short shrift and is deemed unimportant or touchy-feely. But this imbalance has been shifting recently. While emotions still get underweighted in many discussions between investment advisors and their clients, the conversation has improved over the past twenty years. (Throughout this book I'll use the labels investment advisor and investment manager interchangeably.)

Two fields of research have helped shift this focus. The first field is known as behavioral economics or behavioral finance—it studies the intersection of finance and psychology. The second field, neuroscience, examines how the brain functions (or sometimes doesn't function that well) based on new discoveries and the evolution of the brain.

We'll start this chapter with the science of how your brain deals with math and emotions. Then I'll summarize humans' most significant sources of fear and anxiety regarding investing and how best to confront these emotions. Finally, we'll look at how this discomfort can lead us to long for someone who can soothe our anxiety, regardless of whether they actually can.

The Importance of How the Brain Works

When academics began studying investing in the 1950s, their breakthroughs came from applying a scientific approach, including advanced mathematics and—even more importantly—statistics, all made possible with better computers. As they began to understand the relationship between risk and return, they developed quantitative theories and more sophisticated formulas and explanations (though sometimes incomplete or imperfect) that boosted general investment knowledge.

Around the year 2000, this research began to include the study of human behavior, expanding into a new field of finance called either behavioral economics (a broader term) or behavioral finance (more limited to investing). This field of research posits that understanding how your brain works can lead to superior investment decisions.

The early researchers in the 1950s and '60s assumed—without a lot of explicit discussion—that risk and return reflect two conflicting emotions driving investment behavior: fear and greed. However, wealth advisors avoid these latter terms for a couple of reasons. First those terms don't sound like they're grounded in scientific methodology. Second, these emotions have negative connotations. Imagine telling a new client that they're driven by their fear and greed. It sounds almost accusatory.

However, these two emotions are primary factors when it comes to making investment decisions. Let's dig a little deeper into understanding them.

In the 1950s and '60s, around the same time that portfolio theory began, advances in neuroscience shed light on how emotions and thoughts get processed in various parts of the brain, including a region known as the amygdala. Even older in origin than the dinosaurs, this ancient structure has endured for ages across many species. In humans it sits near the top of the spinal column, where it acts as the source of the fight or flight response.

The amygdala helped ensure survival tens of millions of years ago, providing the response needed for the ancestors of what are now contemporary humans to flee in panic upon hearing the roar of a predator. As these ancestors kept evolving, their brains got larger and fancier, and sections like the neocortex—where the serious and most impressive analytic work takes place—grew in both size and function.

So why can't we just make decisions from our neocortex and ignore our amygdala? In the early days of portfolio theory, that's exactly what economists presumed. It's called the *rational actor* concept, which posits that investors act rationally in their own best interests and choose optimal outcomes. Oh, if only it were so easy.

What financial economists and practitioners like my wealth manager friend have found is that the amygdala[1] kicks in and dominates things even when it might be *against* our own best interest. In fact, there's an expression in psychology called *amygdala hijacking*, a fancy term for when our behavior is driven by intense emotion and fear, even if the actual situation doesn't present as much danger as a predator in the wild.

To state the obvious, sometimes we throw tantrums, panic, or act in irrational or counterproductive ways. Let's look at three primal fears around money that can trigger a strong reaction in the amygdala.

Primal Investment Fear #1: Market Collapse

The first and most obvious investment fear is losing money in the stock market or any other risky asset class. When this fear becomes irrational, behavioral economists label it as *loss aversion*, which means a drop in investment value causes more discomfort and emotional pain than a similar increase causes joy. For example, a 20 percent drop in a portfolio triggers two to three times more suffering than a 20 percent increase produces elation. These observations don't come as a great surprise to those of us who remember how awful it felt to lose more than half the value of our stocks in the terrible bear market back in 2008 to 2009.

Unfortunately, there isn't a magic silver bullet to allay this fear, as it's simply part of investing. In fact, if you were to ask me how to look at risk and return in the big picture, I would respond that the stock market or any other risky asset class pays you for the strength of your stomach lining. If you can endure the roller coaster ride of up-and-down markets, you get paid for it in higher returns over the long term.

This conclusion has proven correct over many market ups and downs over the past century. However, it doesn't provide any guarantees about the future, which has a maddening tendency not to look the same as the past. Thus, enduring the discomfort and suffering of watching your portfolio shrink can earn you a higher return over time. The challenge lies in remembering to be disciplined in down markets, which means preventing your amygdala from hijacking your portfolio.

In the investment world, wealth managers talk a lot about *risk tolerance*, a useful term to describe how well an investor can endure market drops without selling out. Risk tolerance shouldn't be measured by how unhappy a down market makes you, but how likely you are to sell out in a panic during an extreme market drop. For example, when I speak with investors who held stocks during the 2008–2009 financial meltdown, I don't ask them if the average drop of over 50 percent in their stock portfolios made them unhappy. That decline made us all unhappy, even those who claim to understand risk. Those who held onto their stocks and never sold, in spite of the fact that it looked like capitalism itself might collapse, showed discipline in rough times and have solid risk tolerance.

During market downturns, math and analysis may not help as much as investors would like, especially since investment managers on average can't predict these stomach-lurching market drops or the recoveries we hope will follow them. However, understanding how your mind reacts to turmoil can help. Knowing in advance that your amygdala will try to dominate can help you let your neocortex keep your amygdala from ruining not just your emotional state but also your financial future.

How likely is it that you'll face the pain of market drops in the future? The Securities and Exchange Commission doesn't allow investment advisors to guarantee anything, since the future of market returns is by definition unknown. However, at some point in an investor's extended time in the stock market, a painful drop in value is pretty much guaranteed. (Nonetheless, at every serious market lurch, there's outcry about how such a thing wasn't supposed to happen.) The problem is that we don't know when these drops will happen, so our amygdala triggers the fear response over and over again.

What's the best way for you to respond to the fear of market collapse? In addition to bracing yourself, it helps to understand that behavior can often be more important than analysis. As Morgan Housel argues in *The Psychology of Money*,[2] it's good behavior, like sticking to your guns in a rough market, that provides the key to successful investment results, more so than good analysis.

Primal Investment Fear #2: Running Out of Money

A second big fear concerns whether or not we'll have enough money to support the lifestyle we want and our other financial needs, like college for our children. Those fears can depend on the magnitude of our total wealth, but even the very wealthy still do financial planning. While someone worth $50 million doesn't have to worry about funding their retirement or paying for their kids' college, the wealthy still worry about funding their lifestyles, their philanthropy, or their eventual bequests to their heirs.

Unlike with the fear of a market collapse, a little math *can* help address the anxiety over running out of money. We can't predict the future (as much as we want to), so this fear can never be eliminated, but with sound financial planning you'll know how likely it is that you'll eventually outspend your portfolio.

Math can't provide perfect investment choices (all this talk about your brain probably clued you into that), but it can provide great benefit when you learn to think *probabilistically*. This means that you can assess the likelihood of various future outcomes, like running out of money or not, based on the odds rather than pretend you know for certain. Gamblers understand probability, like knowing that on a roulette wheel they face a 50 percent chance of either red or black coming up (ignoring the green "zero" slots that make the casino money) or that they have a one-in-thirteen chance of drawing an ace from a complete deck of cards.

Unfortunately for your emotions, though, a probability analysis may provide answers that make you unhappy, like learning that you aren't saving enough money to fund your financial goals or you're spending more than your income supports—an easy trap for us all. Increasing your level of savings may sound easy in self-help books, but in practice it can prove challenging, just like eating a healthier diet or getting more exercise. We may all aspire to versions of those goals, but actually changing behaviors is difficult, especially when our actions don't match our aspirations or self-image. (Mine often don't!)

This book won't help you much to assuage a fear of running out of money, but many online financial planning tools can. (See patrickgeddes.co/transparent-investing for some examples.) In addition, while throughout this book I may criticize investment managers for selling services where we don't add value, many wealth advisors and financial planners do provide a lot of benefit when it comes to forecasting how likely you are to run out of money, irrespective of your total wealth.

Primal Investment Fear #3: Getting Ripped Off by the Investment Industry

Knowing some of the analysis and math of investing can help you deal with advisors, but it doesn't turn you into a well-informed consumer. That's why, in parts 2 and 3 of this book, we'll learn the best ways to interact with investment advisors and distinguish between valuable services and questionable ones. Equally, if not more, important is understanding what motivates advisors and how they get paid, which we'll address in detail.

Savvy, empowered consumers of investment services face a balancing act regarding how cynical they should be when dealing with advisors. Dismissing the entire industry as a rip-off can keep an empowered and well-informed consumer from benefitting from financial advice. However, naïvely believing every promise from an industry trying to sell you on its prowess and integrity can get you into a lot of trouble. In an open letter to Berkshire Hathaway shareholders, renowned investor Warren Buffet once quipped about poker, "If you've been in the game 30 minutes and you don't know who the patsy is, you're the patsy."[3]

While this book delivers a healthy dose of skepticism, the fact remains that investment advisors can provide a great deal of value in dispensing advice and money management services. However, the key here is to avoid either extreme when it comes to trust.

Longing for Daddy

While these primal fears reflect real challenges, they can also lead to the unrealistic expectation that someone else can make the problems go away. Using a cultural gender stereotype as an analogy, we crave a father figure who makes us feel secure and protected.

For the first two fears, market collapse and running out of money, investors may seek to assuage their anxieties by turning to experts for help—a natural reaction. Many aspects of money can trigger strong psychological and emotional reactions in us, and investment managers can provide valid services like hand-holding, education, and portfolio construction that appropriately reassure us. However, investment managers aren't magicians, and they generally can't help in predicting certain outcomes, like big market declines. As we'll cover in part 3 of this book, investment managers can promise or imply a false sense of comfort, and the advisor–client relationship is a nuanced mixture of impulses that sometimes conflict. Understanding these nuances helps you get the best value out of what you pay to investment managers while avoiding false promises.

As a finance professor I know once said, when it comes to investing, "people just want Daddy." Longing for this reassuring presence reflects humans' natural preference for safety, and in many situations, investment managers can provide substantive reassurance. However, it's critical that you understand when the selling of such reassurance is warranted based on data and when it's a false promise driven by the investment industry's greed.

On the positive side, investment managers increasingly turn to the research on behavioral finance as they advise clients and provide reassurance. According to a survey of investment advisors published in *Financial Advisor* magazine in 2020,[4] 81 percent of advisors apply behavioral finance, up from 71 percent the previous year.

A New Science of Fear and Greed

Starting in the 1990s, some economists studying investments started becoming more skeptical of the rational actor model that became popular in the '60s. They didn't prove the entire original theory wrong, but the older model started to look incomplete given how investors don't act all that rationally in practice. Thus, behavioral finance evolved into a field that studied particular human foibles categorized by irrational bias.

This research[5] found evidence of dozens of biases in investing, many of which affect human behavior across many aspects of life. They include:

- Confirmation bias: The tendency to seek only information that supports what we already believe
- Loss aversion: A distorted overweighting of the emotional impact of losses versus the same amount of gain
- Hindsight: Presuming inaccurately that we predicted a past event when in fact we had no idea it was coming

- Recency: A distorted focus on whatever happened recently, say within the last six months, rather than looking at trends over longer time periods
- Overconfidence: An inaccurate assessment of our own skills at investing
- Illusion of control: The belief that we control things that are actually outside of our control

When behavioral finance first documented these biases, investors sought techniques to outsmart the market based on these distortions. Investment managers responded, and many are now incorporating these ideas into how they manage portfolios—or, more accurately, how they manage their clients to help them avoid these traps.

Professionals can provide a lot of value in helping you avoid biases like these that can harm your portfolio, but you can also learn how to manage this behavior on your own. In the next chapter, we'll focus on the bias I consider the most important and harmful: the illusion of control.

Chapter 2

The Illusion of Control, or How Epictetus Would Choose a Broccoli Portfolio

THE HUMAN STRUGGLE with how much of our destiny we actually control has a long and illustrious history across many centuries of philosophy and religion. Buddhism has counseled us for well over two thousand years that we should focus on the things we can control, like our minds, rather than the things we can't control (like the stock market, although the Buddha never stated it quite that way).

The ancient Greek and Roman philosophers known as the Stoics pointed out the same thing. The Stoic philosopher Epictetus advised that our happiness depends on worrying about only the things we can control and not worrying about the rest.[6] The well-known Serenity Prayer from the twentieth century also captures this concept well, as it asks the divine to "grant me the serenity to accept the things I cannot change, courage to change the things I can, and wisdom to know the difference."[7] While these might sound like odd sources of investment advice, they provide excellent grounding for being real about what's feasible.

As humans, we tend to feel happier when we can control our environment. In studies of work environments, employee job satisfaction often correlates with the amount of control employees have over their work.[8] As children, we long for the day when we can do whatever we want. In a way, though, the reality of investing wraps a wet blanket around our longing to control our destiny because the research overwhelmingly shows that neither investors nor their wealth managers show a consistent ability to beat the stock market or accurately predict whether it will go up or down over the short term.

As an investor, you can learn to acknowledge the uncomfortable reality that you can't control outcomes as much as you'd like. The trickier belief to overcome, however, is that by letting go of what you can't control, you're surrendering to fate instead of figuring out how to succeed in beating the market.

Assumptions about what can and can't be controlled form the core of the debate around passive versus active investment (indexing versus active management). Many investors believe that, just like in many parts of life, actively striving for the greener grass on the other side of the hill will lead to great achievements, breakthroughs, and victories. When it comes to investing, however, it's critical to avoid presuming you control more than you do, but much of the investment industry happily encourages that illusion since it makes the industry more money.

As the Serenity Prayer suggests, when picking your battles, you need the wisdom to tell the difference between what you can control and what you can't.

As we saw in the previous chapter, one of the human biases identified by researchers in behavioral finance has appropriately been labelled the *illusion of control*.[9] Those studies have shown that, as investors, we tend to behave as though we wield control over what ends up being a random process. Similarly, these researchers have identified a related bias known as *overconfidence*, proving that we all tend to overestimate our skill at investing. Put together, these two tendencies mean that we harm our financial future by pretending we can control and predict the future better than we can.

For those of us in the male portion of the human population, the research about how skilled we are at investing becomes even more upsetting. A number of researchers, including the authors of one cleverly titled academic article, "Boys Will Be Boys,"[10] have found that women tend to achieve slightly better investment outcomes on average. The reason for this? Men tend to have more unfounded confidence in their abilities. (I imagine this won't be shocking news to women anywhere.)

While the above studies reflect that both genders (on average) lack skills at picking stocks or timing the stock market, women have the advantage of being more honest with themselves about not knowing what's going to happen, whereas men tend to display confidence that doesn't turn out to be justified.

Those results mirror research from outside the realm of investing that suggests that testosterone levels correlate with poorer decision-making due to overconfidence. In fact, one study found that women who were given testosterone showed worse decision-making when it depended on accurately predicting the future.[11] In another study, male options traders who were given testosterone overbid when buying and thus suffered worse financial performance. Those with extra testosterone were also more likely to attribute positive outcomes to skill rather than luck.[12]

Active Management of Ourselves

So why should you as an investor care about the illusion of control or overconfidence? The answer lies in a story I heard at an investment conference. A behavioral finance professor who originally trained in psychology shared that when people find out he studies how investors behave, they often ask, "Can you teach me how to make money in the stock market by capitalizing on other people's biases?" They then become crestfallen when he replies that the real value in behavioral finance lies in looking in the mirror and learning how to avoid your own worst tendencies.

This concept has been understood for a long time, for example by Benjamin Graham, a well-known investor from the mid-twentieth century who helped to popularize the stock research behind active management. In his words, "The investor's chief problem—and even his worst enemy—is likely to be himself."[13]

Conventional wisdom holds that successful investing depends on careful research of financial assets and how markets behave. While investors do need knowledge of, say, the basic differences between stocks and bonds, they have a lot more control (at least theoretically) over their own emotions.

Self-control improves investment performance not in a gratifying way, where we impress our friends with our investment prowess, but in the real payoff that comes from improved returns. The more we avoid making behavioral mistakes based on fear or greed, the larger our investment portfolio becomes. This may sound easy in normal times, but it requires great discipline when it looks as though all of capitalism may implode and our amygdala goes haywire, reflecting the millions of years of evolution behind it.

You may think that I, with all my experience in quantitative risk modeling and studying investor behavior, have achieved some sort of investment Nirvana in which, even during market collapses, I calmly watch the world falling apart like a Zen master. On the contrary. During nasty bear markets, I, too, feel awful and wonder if the economy and stock market will ever recover. The trick lies not in *feeling good* during a bad period, but rather in making sure you don't panic and sell out.

In 2009, during the worst of the crash, a client asked me how I managed to not sell out. I responded—somewhat sheepishly—that while I'd prefer to think that all my experience with risk had given me the discipline to ride things out, the fact was that selling out would mean I was a complete hypocrite. After years of offering clients advice on how to persevere during a downturn, I had to take my own advice. In that way, my self-image helped save me from selling out myself (and, by consequence, selling myself out).

The second way that self-control leads to a bigger portfolio comes from the greed part of our thinking around money—specifically, by avoiding the allure of market-beating performance that sounds sexy but proves hard to achieve. Just like sticking it out in down markets, avoiding the false promise of consistently beating the market requires serious discipline.

What Parts of Investing Can Be Controlled? (Versus the Parts We'd Like to Control)

Just because the evolution of our brain has left some blind spots doesn't mean we've somehow lost our ability to reason or make good decisions. Yet documented biases like the illusion of control set us up for behavioral patterns that aren't ideal for decision-making.

I sometimes put a spin on the phrase "hazardous for your health" by saying that "your brain is hazardous to your wealth."

But health—especially how we eat—is actually a good analogy for how we invest. One could argue that many modern health problems related to diet stem from the now wide availability of the foods our brains evolved to crave millions of years ago. Before the advent of organized agricultural production, our hunter-gatherer ancestors survived, in part, based on their cravings for sweet or fatty foods, which provided a higher dose of much-needed calories. Unfortunately, that hard-wiring of the brain now leads to problems like obesity, since fatty and sweet foods are widely available in the developed world.

This food analogy extends into the two main—and competing—approaches to investing, which I like to call Chocolate Cake versus Broccoli.[14]

Imagine two plates in front of you: one is a piece of chocolate cake; the other is a piece of broccoli. Which do you want to take a bite of? Chances are, you want the cake (and if you didn't choose it because you don't like chocolate, or cake in general, swap it out for your favorite treat and try the exercise again).

Even though the neocortex may rationally calculate that eating the broccoli might keep us alive longer, everyone knows from their own experience that such rational thoughts often lose out to primal cravings. We can't seem to stop ourselves as we reach for the cake.

When investing, you face this same tension between the part of your brain that longs for the sweet and satisfying versus the rational (and often boring) part that chooses based on actual data.

Chocolate Cake Investing

The Chocolate Cake mindset toward investing presumes that we control much of our own destiny when it comes to how our portfolios actually perform. It appeals to a romantic narrative about investing, in which smart people beat the stock market through shrewd insights and knowledge. Unfortunately, it doesn't reflect reality all that well, but we'll get to that issue later. To illustrate the difference between the Chocolate Cake mindset and the Broccoli mindset, we'll focus on four key parts of investing: return, risk, fees, and taxes.

If you ask Chocolate Cake investors to rank these four items by which they intuitively believe matters most, they'll put them in the following order.

Table 1. Chocolate Cake Mindset

Component	Rationale
Return	Duh—who wouldn't rank this first? It's the part that affects our wealth. It's also the sexy part of investing and the part everyone talks about the most.

Risk	Investors have known since the 1950s and '60s that risk matters, although this awareness took some time to gain traction.
Fees	In the period from 2000 to 2020, costs began to be broadly recognized as a significant predictor of returns.[15] Fees had been viewed as boring, but now a lot of investors are waking up to their importance.
Taxes	If fees are boring, the tax impact of different ways to invest is mind-numbingly, eyes-glazed-over boring—not to mention that taxes are intimidating to understand when it comes to how they affect various investment strategies.

Many investors reflect the Chocolate Cake mindset when they invest, and the investment industry loves to support, if not exploit, this viewpoint, since these beliefs increase the industry's revenue. Just as food advertisers know how to hit your hot buttons regarding tasty food, the investment industry shows great skill at appealing to the romantic thrill of beating the market while hoping you'll ignore how badly their overall efforts to do so have turned out over time.

The ranking above also reflects how our brains have evolved in that this kind of thinking served us well thousands of years ago when humans were still trying to figure out which parts of the universe and which outcomes they actually controlled. (Early humans often presumed that their actions affected things like celestial bodies.) The development of scientific thinking, especially over the past four centuries, has helped clarify which things we control and which we don't, although we continue to long for more control than we actually have.

Broccoli Investing

Let's turn now to the Broccoli mindset, which reflects research and data rather than the illusion of control. This approach takes the same four components and uses statistical evidence to rank them from most to least control.

A Broccoli investor ranks these four items in the following order (and if this interpretation of reality doesn't feel as appealing as Chocolate Cake, remember that your brain is wired to prefer the cake).

Table 2. Broccoli Mindset

Component	Rationale
Fees	What we pay the investment industry is the factor we have the most control over. This doesn't mean cheaper is always better, but it's the most important and predictable explanation of investment success.
Taxes	Taxes aren't as easy to control as fees, but their impact on investment returns turns out to be pretty consistent over time. Of course, taxes may not matter in an account like a Roth 401(k), but for taxable investments they matter enormously, especially for those with high incomes who pay the highest tax rates.

Risk	The risk (i.e., the fear component) of most investments tends to remain fairly consistent over time, although strategies or asset classes that have been relatively safe in the past can suddenly show that they're much riskier than investors presumed.
Return	Disappointingly, the part we most want to control has been shown over time to be the most random.

Rewiring Our Brains

From an evolutionary perspective, we're just as hard-wired to crave market-beating performance as we are fatty and sweet foods. This hard-wiring makes it particularly difficult to shift our preferences to indexing (passive investing), the boring and unromantic broccoli in this scenario.

The "sugar rush" of beating the market and making a killing sounds emotionally appealing, but unfortunately, the evidence shows that the odds are overwhelmingly stacked against us. This doesn't mean there have never been brilliant investment managers who happen to beat the market—in any historical period, you'll find people who've successfully outperformed. Instead, the challenge lies in how good you are, or how good investment managers are, at predicting which active managers will succeed in the future.

Claiming that all active management should be defined as foolish is too extreme. However, the natural inclination of investors who aren't as familiar with the historical inability of the industry to achieve its claims is to default to *performance chasing*, or firing underperforming managers and moving that money to ones who have been performing better.

I'm not arguing that all active management should be shunned, but that every investor should default to a passive indexing approach first and maintain a high level of wariness around any claims of being able to beat the market. In other words, chocolate cake isn't poison, but over the long term, a diet of mainly chocolate cake and very little broccoli will likely lead to a shorter life expectancy on average.

Given how your brain works, overcoming cravings like the ones for beating the market or eating that slice of chocolate cake can be difficult. Simply understanding that broccoli will lead to a longer life expectancy doesn't make it easier to change your behavior around eating. Similarly, changing your assumptions about investing will take discipline, patience, and education—especially education on how poorly asset managers have actually fared in trying to beat the market and on how your brain works. Your emotional longings shouldn't be viewed as an enemy to be vanquished or shamed, but rather as a part of your own human reality to be understood (yet not necessarily appointed to manage your investments).

With this, remember that investment advisors are people too, with emotions, biases, and the same flaws as everyone else. The vast majority of advisors are not trying to swindle innocent investors, but, like all humans, they are motivated by self-interest. It certainly doesn't help that the investment industry doesn't have a great track record for fully disclosing the areas where we do add value versus where we've slid into the realm of pushing strategies and products more likely to enrich us than our clients.

As a way to strengthen your skills at spotting when you're being offered chocolate cake instead of broccoli, we'll turn next to what I call investment myths. Like the illusion of control, these myths can cause real harm to the value of your portfolio.

Chapter 3

Myth Busting

FIVE HARMFUL preconceived beliefs, or myths, about investing can lead you to make poor investment choices. These are, effectively, the practical implications of how your brain can be hazardous to your wealth. All five of these myths represent traps in the form of inaccurate assumptions about how both investing and the investment industry actually work. The more you're aware of these traps and can avoid succumbing to them, the more empowered you'll be to make better choices that improve your financial situation. And remember, the investment industry makes a lot more money from investors who believe in these myths, so advisors aren't always on your side when it comes to debunking them.

Myth #1: Hire the Wizard with the Best Crystal Ball

I once gave a small seminar on investing to about fifteen people gathered in someone's living room. A woman there shared her concern that she wanted "someone who knew what was coming" to be in charge of her portfolio. I responded with sympathy about her anxiety at not knowing how markets would behave and confirmed that she was right in thinking she didn't know what the future held. I then asked her, "But why do you want to pay a lot of money to an investment advisor who has no more idea than you do of what the future will bring?"

Turning back to how our brains work, we tend to presume we have the ability to predict all sorts of outcomes beyond our actual capabilities to do so. Then, after the fact, we think, "I knew it all along," or, "I saw that coming from a mile away." Behavioral finance researchers call this *hindsight* bias, in which we assume that something could have been predicted when it was, in fact, what statisticians call a probabilistic outcome—a fancy way of saying it was random and outside of our control. Finance researchers aren't the only ones who've figured out the pitfalls of assuming we know more about an outcome in advance than we do. Gamblers, who operate in a world of probabilities, also offer insights into the dangers of certain kinds of self-deception.

Remember Annie Duke, the professional gambler, who argued that the key to better decisions lies in thinking about life's challenges as more like poker than like chess? Well, the investment industry wants consumers to think of investing as more like chess, meaning that, naturally, you need to hire the best grandmasters to skillfully guide you.

Duke describes the pitfalls of a human behavior she calls *resulting*, which is when we judge the quality of a decision based on its outcome rather than on whether it was a good decision at the time.[16] As an example, she talks about an infamous football play at the end of Super Bowl XLIX, when the New England Patriots intercepted a pass near their own goal line, which led to their surprise victory over the Seattle Seahawks. The press overwhelmingly excoriated the Seahawks coach, Pete Carroll, as having made the worst decision in Super Bowl history by choosing to pass on that play, but Coach Carroll said that even though the outcome of the decision had been a disaster, the decision itself wasn't a bad one given the probabilities, which supported his choice. "Monday morning quarterbacking"— criticizing something after the event—is an example of resulting that applies perfectly to investing as well.

For those who favor passive investing, the distinction between decisions and outcomes has proved insightful over the years. For example, let's say I'm deciding today how much of my portfolio to put in stocks and how much to put in bonds. I know that the best decision reflects both my current financial situation and the fact that in the long term, stocks have historically paid much higher returns than bonds but at much higher risk in the form of short-term fluctuations.

Let's say I'm deciding between a more aggressive portfolio of 80 percent stocks and 20 percent bonds versus a more tame portfolio of 60 percent stocks and 40 percent bonds.

Well, if the stock market outperforms bonds over the next five years, the 80/20 portfolio will look like it was a better decision (hindsight bias). However, if stocks perform worse than bonds over those five years, the 60/40 portfolio will seem like it was the better choice, as seen in this table.

Table 3. Hindsight Bias Illustrated

Outcome in 5 Years	Best Choice with Hindsight Bias
Stocks perform better than bonds	80% Stocks/20% Bonds
Bonds perform better than stocks	60% Stocks/40% Bonds

Since I can't know in advance whether the stock market will do better over the next five years, this simple comparison is a terrible way to judge success.

Furthermore, an unpredictable bad market for stocks over five years doesn't mean the 80/20 portfolio is a bad choice if I have a very long time horizon and can endure rough markets and persevere. Similarly, if I have a shorter time horizon or not as much stomach for risk, the 60/40 portfolio may be the best choice—even if stocks outperform bonds over the next five years.

Good investment decisions are often inappropriately judged in hindsight to be the ones that made the most money. I argue that the best investment decisions reflect an investor's particular situation and goals *at the time the decision was made.*

Table 4. Hindsight Bias vs. Best Choice Today

Outcome in 5 Years	Best Choice with Hindsight Bias	Best Actual Choice Today
Stocks perform better than bonds	80% Stocks/20% Bonds	Depends on investor's time horizon and risk tolerance
Bonds perform better than stocks	60% Stocks/40% Bonds	Depends on investor's time horizon and risk tolerance

The investment industry has been pushed to acknowledge, reluctantly, that its experts actually have very little success in predicting the future, but it still likes to pretend it can predict more accurately than it can. Adding to this resistance, the clients of the industry, like you, often prefer the worldview that brilliant experts do exist and that those experts can make a killing for their clients through shrewd and unique foresight. All you have to do is find them.

While amazing successes do occur from time to time across the entire industry and all the dollars managed professionally, the average expert who tries to outsmart the market usually proves more effective at outsmarting their clients.

So, if we aren't able to accurately predict the future or out-smart the market, isn't investing really just a form of gambling? After all, investing, like gambling, presents us with unknown outcomes. However, two major differences exist.

First, gambling at casinos presents what mathematicians call a *negative expected return* for the gamblers. This means that if many people gamble at a casino many times, the payoffs are calculated so the house (the casino) wins a slight profit over time and gamblers overall have a slight negative return.

By contrast, investing has a *positive* expected return over long time horizons across many investors. (However, it still pays to scrutinize how much the house makes, i.e., the invest-ment industry. We'll look more closely at fees in a later chapter.)

The second big difference between investing and gambling comes back to Annie Duke's comment that winning at poker requires both skill and luck, based on the fact that the best gam-blers exhibit real ability to win beyond what the odds would predict. If I were to play many games of poker against a high-end professional gambler, I'd probably get lucky and win a few hands, but over the long haul, their skill would lead to my losing the vast majority of the time. In short, their skill enables them to win more often.

Active investment management, however, doesn't work this way, considering that even a novice can outperform an expert if the novice chooses passive investing and the expert chooses active investing. Based on actual results, skill in the investment industry hasn't provided the same advantage as it does in poker.

So what's the best way to escape the myth of the wizard with a crystal ball? Keep reminding yourself that it's false to believe that investment managers, on average, can predict the future accurately. Even though clinging to this myth may soothe your anxieties, it can lead to poor investment choices, such as betting on outperformance.

And in terms of hiring an investment expert, don't presume that this is akin to hiring either a professional poker player or a chess grandmaster to help you win the game. Unlike in poker and chess, in which expert-level skill does lead to consistent outperformance, the skill to outperform or time the market is so rare it's not worth betting on.

Myth #2: Successful Investing Requires Spending a Lot of Time

In the Chocolate Cake world that we explored in chapter 2, investors and the managers they hire focus on the returns of an investment, which unfortunately turns out to be the most random of the four investment components (return, risk, fees, taxes).

This mindset presumes that the more research an investor or manager does, the higher the return. This belief makes perfect sense, until we look at the overwhelming results of decades of research, which show that returns are uncontrollable and inconsistent, regardless of how much time an investor spends researching and analyzing the market.

As an investor, you may assume that hiring an expert is similar to hiring someone to clean your house. Cleaning a house takes time, since self-cleaning homes remain science fiction, so someone has to put in the hours. When you pay a housecleaner to put in that time so you don't have to, you know that the amount of time they spend working for you will result in achieving your initial goal: a clean house. However, with investment managers, the time to research and gaze into a crystal ball doesn't pay off, so it's time that shouldn't be delegated in the same way you might delegate housework. In other words, it's an illusion that successful investing automatically requires a lot of time.

Followers of the Broccoli mindset accept that beating or timing the market is effectively out of our control and not predictable, which means that the time requirement for researching the best portfolio and monitoring it on an ongoing basis suddenly plummets. A simple portfolio of index funds or their equivalent can be set up and then forgotten, for the most part, while still yielding profitable returns.

A colleague of mine at Aperio Group interviewed Bill Sharpe many years ago for an investment guide my colleague was writing. In the 1960s, Sharpe, a Nobel laureate in economics, came up with the Capital Asset Pricing Model, or CAPM, one of the most important and well-known breakthroughs in investment theory. My colleague asked Sharpe how often he thought investors should look at their portfolios. Sharpe's immediate answer was five years. Then he corrected himself and said, "No, you can't tell people they need to look at their portfolios only every five years—you'd better say three years."

Even I don't recommend something this infrequent (I advise investors to look at their portfolios once a year). But Sharpe's original suggestion for five years actually works fine in terms of the math.

Many people react with shock when they hear how little time I recommend spending on feeding and caring for their portfolio, but staying on top of market news, research, and new developments just doesn't provide enough value to make all that work worthwhile. In fact, constantly checking your portfolio can lead to lower returns because it can encourage excessive trading—a cost that comes from overconfidence.

The myth that investing requires spending a lot of time implies that the best investors stay on top of fast-breaking news, perhaps by watching financial news networks on TV. Cynics like me refer to such programming as financial pornography, as the real goal turns out to be titillation.

Remember how many investors (especially the male variety) presume they can outsmart the market? That same presumption drives the erroneous belief that spending lots of research time will pay off.

In so much of life, the harder we work to prepare for a task, the more successful the outcome—be it a student practicing a musical instrument, an actor preparing for a movie role, or an Olympic athlete training. In investing, the Serenity Prayer's lesson lies in accepting what we can and can't control and having the wisdom to tell the difference. This doesn't mean that educating yourself on basic investment concepts is a waste of time, but it does undercut a major industry promise that investment managers can predict the future.

Myth #3: Good Investments Need to Be Complicated

Part of the myth, and allure, of the shrewd investment manager beating the market rests on the assumption that simple solutions are for simpletons—in other words, that really smart investors should have more complicated portfolios.

Not all complicated investment strategies are bad by any means. But the danger with these strategies is that investors may not fully understand what they're really getting. Economists have a fancy term for the difficulty consumers face when the people selling them something know a lot more about the product or service than the consumers do: *information asymmetry*. Basically, consumers face a tougher time making the best decisions for themselves when they're not as clear on the full picture as those selling to them.

Arguably, many industries *prefer* their new customers to be naïve, because it's harder to sell to informed consumers. The investment industry is no different. However, the information asymmetry in investing can represent a pretty big gap, and that's why it pays to be wary about how we investment managers pitch our services. While we can help clients manage risk and earn higher returns, we don't do it by our predictive abilities. Thus, the asymmetry hurts investors when their advisors say, "This stuff is complicated, so please leave it to the experts." Parts of investing can be complicated and warrant serious analysis. However, when complexity becomes a way to sell predictive abilities or distract clients, that complexity can harm their portfolios. Wizards behind curtains are good at intimidation.

The myth that good investing requires complexity presents some tricky nuance, however, since parts of investing can be quite complicated. At Aperio Group, we've offered extremely complicated quantitative strategies and prided ourselves on our sophisticated analysis of risk and tax economics—thus, I'd be a hypocrite if I claimed that complexity automatically represents untrustworthy motives. Instead, consumers should be aware that complexity is sometimes used as a way to impress less sophisticated investors and justify higher fees.

Simple doesn't equate to ineffective or sub-optimal. Some investors mistrust a solution as simple as building a collection of index funds, but the smartest investors (followers of the

Broccoli mindset) prove again and again that this boring and simple solution has better results on average.

Investors assume that if they're shelling out money for an advisor, they deserve to be dazzled. After all, if you hired a professional chef to come into your home and cook for your dinner party, you'd feel pretty ripped off if you caught them preparing macaroni and cheese out of a box. With the chef, you'd be justified in feeling rooked, but with an investment manager, you're more in danger of getting hoodwinked by an investment strategy that's too fancy than by one that's too simple.

Myth #4: Shrewd Investing Requires a Lot of Activity (or the Appearance of Activity)

When I ran the research department at Morningstar, a wealth advisor told me that his clients needed to see regular small tweaks in their portfolios. At one point in time, when foreign stocks happened to be down for a few months, he said his clients were asking him if they should get out of that asset class. He knew he wasn't going to be effective at timing when foreign stocks were going to outperform domestic stocks, or vice versa. Thus, he didn't want to change his clients' allocations. However, he shared, they needed to see some sort of activity to reassure them of his value, so he found a different foreign stock mutual fund and switched to it, keeping the allocation the same.

Remember when we talked about the human brain and how we crave control over the future? And that feeling like we aren't in control can trigger a fear response from the amygdala? When investors hire a wealth manager, they crave the illusion that someone is in control. They feel more comfortable when they see activity, as it seems to indicate that the manager is on top of what's going on, whether that's true or not.

They've bought into the myth the investment industry wants them to believe: that shrewd investing means seeing a lot of activity in their portfolios.

This misconception puts pressure on investment managers, and many avoid revealing their limitations (that they don't know which stocks are more likely to outperform) because they fear their clients won't stick with them. While I would always recommend a more honest approach (confessing that we don't know which stock is going to outperform), the realities of doing this are challenging when clients and the investment industry as a whole believe the myth.

Another wealth advisor articulated this dance perfectly by saying that his clients mistook activity for cleverness and that wealth managers need to show activity to retain clients (though he was honorable not to pander to his clients like that). When he told me this, I thought of the line, "Don't just do something. Sit there," a concept right out of Buddhism. Even though doing nothing may feel boring and scary, the research has shown it to be the smartest path. Similarly, the assumption that activity proves someone's in control can lead investors to make poor decisions, like fiddling with their portfolio instead of letting it sit untouched.

Think especially of market downturns, when you experience the most panic and fear. At such times, your brain is hard-wired to presume that you need to take action, probably by bailing out of the stock market or other risky asset classes. However, riding through market downturns has proven to be the real key to long-term wealth, since the market pays you for the strength of your stomach lining.

During major market meltdowns, investors naturally need more soothing and reassuring. This often means that, during that panic, their need to see activity on their portfolios grows even stronger. Smart investment managers can play a valuable role at such times by assuring their clients that it's prudent to stay on the right long-term path and that the current troubles will likely pass. This psychological aid does provide real value by talking clients down off the ledge and preventing them from selling at what often turns out to be market bottoms.

However, investment managers can't wave magic wands and make the trouble go away, no matter how much their clients project upon them these supernatural abilities. A good advisor can help you through these bad times but as a coach or therapist, not a wizard consulting a crystal ball.

Myth #5: The Wealthy Know How to Find the Wizard with the Most Accurate Crystal Ball

Speaking of the wizard with a crystal ball, this final myth also arises from the illusion of control. Investors without large sums of money to manage often believe that while they can't hire brilliant managers to beat the market, the very wealthy can.

A woman I know who leads organizations that provide educational content to the ultra-wealthy shared her typical experience with someone who's just come into tens of millions of dollars through selling a successful business. She said their first question usually boils down to how to find the brilliant superstar wealth manager who will provide them with outsize returns. After learning more, these individuals then shift to trying to find the best firm, and then finally they realize they need to start focusing on their goals and expectations first, rather than finding the superstar.

Many of these investors are successful business owners who have shown consummate skill at hiring leaders and experts, so it makes sense that they presume the same approach will work in the investment world. Similarly, they assume that they'll end up being just as successful in outsmarting the stock market as they were in growing their business. (One advisor I know describes such clients as the Masters of the Universe.)

When I work with very wealthy clients, I explain about all the money spent by professional investors in trying to beat the market. Then I ask them if, when they built a successful company, they had to compete with *millions* of competitors around the globe spending tens, if not hundreds, of billions of dollars all trying to do the same thing. In other words, competing in the game of beating the market presents a very different competitive challenge, no matter what our old friend overconfidence likes to whisper in our ear.

However, while the wealthy can't necessarily find the best wizards, they can access certain strategies because of their buying power. Clients with $50 million or more, for example, can access certain types of investments unavailable to those with much smaller portfolios, including a broader set of opportunities in private equity, hedge funds, and real asset partnerships.

But just because these specialized strategies sometimes provide great risk-adjusted returns doesn't mean they're free of the same problems that affect the products smaller investors can access, like mutual funds. The people selling these special strategies are incentivized to focus on the benefits of their offerings, just like investment managers who cater to those with a lot less wealth. And the very wealthy, overall, show the same range of knowledge about investing as those with less wealth and have the same ratio of people who understand how the game is played versus people who are at risk of getting played themselves.

In other words, while the wealthy may avail themselves of more opportunities, the information asymmetry and incentive problems remain just as much a challenge for the rich.

Along the same lines, you might think that big institutional investors like pension funds can spend the money to hire the best managers. But again, the data prove to be uncooperative in supporting this narrative: most big endowments and pension plans get sucked into the same false promises with equally awful results on average.[17]

Hopefully, learning about these myths—as well the influence of your emotions and biases—has helped you see how easily we all fall into psychological traps when it comes to investing. Now, to support you in becoming an even more empowered consumer of investment services, we'll shift the focus from your brain to the brains of the investment managers you might hire.

Part II

THE INVESTMENT INDUSTRY UNVARNISHED

Chapter 4

The Biases and Motivations of Investment Managers

IT SHOULD COME AS NO SURPRISE to anyone that in a capitalist world companies can make more money by building their sales message around consumer psychology. The more a company can manipulate people into doing what it wants (e.g., buying its product), the better its bottom line. Some people see this as sinister. Others believe it's appropriate product or marketing-campaign design. After all, understanding how people behave doesn't have to lead to unethical behavior.

Whatever your level of cynicism, the fact remains that many industries benefit from carefully studying how their clients behave. Think of social media, an industry that's grown exponentially in part because it satisfies a genuine biological longing for connection. For example, research[18] has shown that when a Facebook user gets others to like a post, the user's brain shows increased levels of dopamine, a chemical that drives us to pursue our cravings. Sean Parker, the founding president of Facebook, said in *The Guardian* in 2018 that the platform takes advantage of a "vulnerability in human psychology," adding that liking or commenting on something within the platform provides "a little dopamine hit."[19]

In the gambling industry, the bells and flashing lights on a slot machine are intentionally designed to stimulate the gambler's cravings. In the snack food industry, products are designed to have the ideal mouth feel that will keep consumers purchasing more of their product.

In the investment industry, the promise of financial success and feeling superior by outsmarting other investors is the equivalent of a dopamine hit or the perfect mouth feel. The industry knows that acknowledging that the odds are heavily stacked against beating the market isn't a great way to draw customers. However, consumer awareness has been increasing, and the industry has had to scramble to respond to its clients' becoming warier about how probable those promised dopamine hits really are.

Of course, self-serving narrative spin is likely as old as human language, and we all do it to varying degrees. And it's not breaking the law for an investment manager to claim that their clients might outperform and beat the market, given that it is certainly possible. Nonetheless, it's misleading to ignore the research that overwhelmingly shows how, on average, active managers have *not* beaten it.

Becoming an empowered investor means remaining on guard against how investment managers may try to stimulate our human cravings—like being a disciplined dieter who flips the channel when a seductive ad for junk food comes on. Remember, it's easier to sell chocolate cake than broccoli for a reason. Sometimes we need to indulge our cravings, but we shouldn't pretend that unhealthy fare, whether in food or investment management, is actually good for us.

Cognitive Dissonance, or How the Investment Industry Pretends It's Not Manipulating Your Brain

Researchers in behavioral finance have identified a common bias in investors called *cognitive dissonance*, a term borrowed from broader behavioral psychology.[20] Cognitive dissonance occurs when contradictory behaviors or beliefs clash. The discomfort that arises from this contradiction can lead us to ignore evidence that might help us make a better choice, simply because it conflicts with one of our cravings or desires. When we encounter this kind of internal conflict, we have to bend one of our beliefs or practices, regardless of whether the data support it.

In a study from the 1950s, the psychologist who coined the term cognitive dissonance, Leon Festinger, analyzed a small religious cult that had predicted the end of the world. When the apocalypse uncooperatively failed to arrive on time, a normal reaction might have been for the cult members to change their belief in their ability to foresee it. However, instead of readjusting in the face of overwhelming evidence, the believers doubled down (just as Festinger had predicted), claiming that their faith had postponed the world's demise.[21]

When we're faced with the discomfort of hard evidence, our minds often make up another story to protect our cherished beliefs. Some social and evolutionary psychologists suggest that this is because the neocortex usually tries to rationalize whatever the emotional and subconscious part of the brain craves. Jonathan Haidt, the social psychologist, suggests that the neocortex should be viewed as a presidential press secretary whose job it is to defend and justify whatever the president (the amygdala, with its strong emotions and cravings) does and says.[22]

This trap ensnares both consumers and investment managers equally. Investors can rationalize emotions that lead to bad investment decisions because, in effect, we humans are hardcoded to deceive ourselves about our reasons for how we choose the best investments, which means we conveniently ignore how self-serving the choice of active management might be. We gloss over the reality of failed outperformance, perhaps rationalizing that, while on average the pros fail to beat or predict the market, everyone likes to think of themselves as exceptional.

Then again, we advisors rationalize that the fact that we happen to earn higher fees from active management is just a coincidence, since no one wants to think of themselves as motivated by greed. We pretend to ourselves that we make decisions on our clients' behalf solely from an impartial, rational perspective with their best interests in mind. Sometimes investment pros do confess their actual motivation, like an advisor years ago who told me, "Everyone knows you can't beat the market, but you can't make any money selling indexing."

Behavioral economists have identified a similar pattern of self-deception known as *confirmation bias*. This is when, in seeking evidence to make a decision, we skew heavily toward the evidence that supports what we want to do and tend to ignore any evidence, however persuasive, that doesn't. Like the members of the doomsday cult, our minds often put a cherished or self-serving belief first, and to avoid cognitive dissonance, all evidence must be contorted to fit that belief, however uncooperative the actual data.

In fact, research has shown that when we're looking to confirm something we already believe, we set a low bar and are usually satisfied with a couple of positive references. However, when we're seeking to disprove something we desperately want to be false, we search for justification and pounce on it with satisfaction even if it's, say, the tenth piece of evidence we've examined (having rejected the first nine as flawed since they provided support in the "wrong" direction).[23]

I ran into this problem while working on this book. As I assembled research articles on indexing, I noticed myself becoming suspicious of the ones that ran counter to my assumption about active management—even though the preponderance of data clearly shows that the odds are stacked against outperforming the market. I didn't want to have to confront that contradictory information, despite my awareness of confirmation bias, thus supporting the idea that simply acknowledging our biases and self-deceptions in advance doesn't automatically mean we can always avoid them.

The raging active versus passive debate within the investment industry shows obvious cognitive dissonance. The debate is often depicted as two equally valid arguments grounded in data and evidence, when in practice, the hard numbers only support one side. However, like many controversial debates over the course of human history, the disagreement doesn't get resolved by this actual evidence because if the truth were well understood, it would be a threat to those with something to lose (like higher fees and revenue). Herein lies the cognitive dissonance, since entrenched self-serving interests and beliefs lead us to vociferously resist the facts.

In the seventeenth century, the Roman Catholic Church almost had the scientist Galileo put to death not because they disputed the accuracy of his astronomical observations but because his evidence that the earth wasn't at the center of the universe undercut both their belief system and their authority. In fact, Galileo complained in a letter to fellow astronomer Johannes Kepler about the philosophers who refused to look through his telescope because they were so threatened by what they'd see:

> My dear Kepler, I wish that we might laugh at the remarkable stupidity of the common herd. What do you have to say about the principal philosophers of this academy who are filled with the stubbornness of an asp and do not want to look at either the planets, the moon or the telescope, even though I have freely and deliberately offered them the opportunity a thousand times? Truly, just as the asp stops its ears, so do these philosophers shut their eyes to the light of truth.[24]

I'd argue that many in the investment industry similarly refuse to look at the overwhelming research showing the failures of active management. They, like Galileo's persecutors, have a vested interest in undercutting or invalidating the evidence.

Power and money exert a strong influence on our beliefs. In fact, you could argue that investing as a practice is all about monetary incentive. While investment managers claim to look rationally at the historical data about active investing, their beliefs tend to be heavily skewed by the additional money they can earn by steering their clients to the more expensive active strategies.

The great muckraker Upton Sinclair described it brilliantly when he said, "It is difficult to get a man to understand something, when his salary depends on his not understanding it!"[25] Like the doomsday cult members whose certainty about their ability to predict the end of the world proved to be flawed, active investment managers cling to their story of predictive prowess in spite of the evidence and data that prove otherwise.

Trustworthy Sages or Rip-Off Artists?

When we interact with experts in fields different from our own, we face the challenge of not knowing as much as those people. This is true across many types of experts: doctors, plumbers, lawyers, or car mechanics, for example. This information asymmetry puts consumers at a disadvantage, but it doesn't necessarily mean the expert will act dishonorably. Like any of the experts just listed, investment managers generally want to do right by their clients, but some do exploit their information advantage.

So, should investment experts be viewed as trustworthy sages or rip-off artists? As is frequently the case with difficult choices, the truth lies somewhere between the two extremes.

Over the course of my career, I've encountered the full spectrum of assumptions about investment managers. Some consumers view their advisors with awe, assuming that we're brilliant and trustworthy. While some investment managers may earn this lofty respect, in general, this perception reflects naïveté about what predictive abilities we actually have. Putting wealth advisors up on such a high pedestal falls into the trap of the illusion of control.

On the other hand, I've also encountered cynics who view the entire profession as a bunch of snake oil salespeople offering thinly disguised shams to the unsophisticated. While I remain highly critical of my industry, that extreme view displays just as much oversimplification as the blind-faith version.

So how can consumers protect themselves against self-serving investment managers while not sliding into over-reactive cynicism? I like to use the directive "trust, but verify," which was made famous in the 1980s during arms negotiations between Ronald Reagan and Mikhail Gorbachev. It's also helpful to understand exactly how investment managers get paid.

Chapter 5

How Investment Managers Get Paid

IF YOU WERE TO ASK ME, "Patrick, what's the most important thing in investing?" you might hope for a clever insight on how to analyze investments in order to make a killing. Sorry to disappoint, but my actual answer is pretty boring: it's fees, meaning what you pay others to manage your money or give you advice.

Why are fees the most important part of investing? Because they're the easiest to control, and they have the most research behind them as being a proven means to boost returns. While fees may seem trivial, even an extra half a percent per year in increased returns can really add up over decades of investing. For example, let's say you invest $100,000 in a stock portfolio that earns 8 percent before fees, but you can choose between one that charges you 0.6 percent per year in fees versus one that charges you only 0.1 percent. After twenty-five years, you'll end up with approximately $73,000 more in the lower-fee version, leaving you more than 10 percent wealthier.

Table 5. Impact of Fees Compounded Over 25 Years

	Starting Balance	Net Annual Return	Ending Balance
High-Fee Strategy	$100,000	8.0%-0.6%=7.4%	$595,809
Low-Fee Strategy	$100,000	8.0%-0.1%=7.9%	$669,169
Advantage from Lower Fees		0.5%	$73,360

It's an exciting time to be preaching about fees, since consumers in the US have moved a lot of their investments out of high-fee strategies and into low-cost index funds. And even beyond indexing, the consumer focus on fees has never been higher—the entire industry is reeling from the pressure to drive down costs.

How exactly will learning about fees help your portfolio earn higher returns? Instead of thinking of investing as maximizing your portfolio, think of your interaction with the investment industry as akin to how you interact with a supermarket or restaurant. Would you shop at a supermarket that didn't have any prices on the shelves or eat at a restaurant with no prices on the menu? Of course not. You wouldn't be able to make an informed choice without understanding the prices. Unfortunately, the investment industry can intentionally make it harder for you to figure out its full pricing.

It's true that learning about fees may be the most unexciting part of investing. It means eating broccoli because you know it's good for you instead of biting into that enticing piece of chocolate cake. But unlike with the sexy and appealing "teach me how to make a killing" Chocolate Cake approach, understanding this math really can improve your portfolio's performance.

Let's start by examining how the industry gets paid for the services it provides.

How You Pay for Two Different Types of Investment Experts

We'll start our study of fees by looking at two distinct types of investment managers: wealth managers and asset managers. Wealth managers work directly with you to structure an overall portfolio and provide what's known as asset allocation, meaning how much of your portfolio should be held in various asset classes, such as domestic stocks, foreign stocks, bonds, cash, real estate, and even more exotic strategies for the wealthy, like private equity and hedge funds. Wealth managers usually provide the big picture in the form of an asset allocation and then oversee the portfolio on an ongoing basis.

Asset managers, on the other hand, implement the strategies chosen by the wealth managers. For example, if your wealth manager allocates 15 percent of your portfolio to real estate, they may hire a real estate asset manager (or a few) on your behalf. These asset managers may then execute the wealth manager's strategy for real estate through a mutual fund of publicly traded real estate stocks known as REITs (real estate investment trusts), or, for very wealthy investors, the wealth advisor might pick a private real estate partnership.

To make a medical analogy, your wealth manager would be your general practitioner while the asset managers would be the medical specialists who focus on narrower health issues like cardiology or ophthalmology.

The distinction between wealth and asset managers isn't always this clear, however, as some advisors play both parts. But often the roles remain separate since a specific asset class like foreign stocks or real estate requires more specialized knowledge than a wealth manager might be expected to have across many types of investments.

Both types of manager need to get paid, and part of your challenge in being an informed consumer lies in figuring out exactly how each professional or company receives their compensation.

Generally, wealth managers are compensated by three basic methods: commissions (including a specific type of commission called a load fee), fees as a percentage of assets, and a flat retainer (or hourly). Asset managers, on the other hand, usually get paid a percentage of the assets they manage, sometimes with an extra fee tied to how well they perform. Let's look at both in more detail.

Wealth Management Fees

The commission model's market share has shrunk, and brokerage firms like Charles Schwab and Fidelity no longer charge commissions on stock trades. However, investors today can still end up paying per-trade commissions to buy stocks or other securities, especially with what are called load mutual funds.

With a load fund, your wealth manager sells you a mutual fund and gets paid out of the *load*, which is an extra fee added on top of the regular expenses paid to the asset manager to run the fund. Here's an example scenario.

Table 6. Example of Load Fees

	Fee Charged Each Year
Operating expense for an average stock mutual fund without extra load	0.90%*
Typical load charged in each of the first five years	1.00%
Total fee, including load	1.90%

*Average fee for US equity load funds. Source: Morningstar US Fund Fee Study, June 2020

Here, you're already paying 0.90 percent for the asset manager's operating expenses for running the fund (retaining the asset manager and paying for any legal and administrative costs). Then, on top of this amount, the wealth manager effectively earns 1.00 percent of your total investment each year for the first five years you hold that fund.

So, you're now paying just under 2 percent per year for five years, after which the load charge typically disappears. In comparison, a low-cost diversified stock index fund typically has a fee between 0.05 percent to 0.15 percent every year. So with a load fund, you're losing an awful lot of your money to pay a lot of different people whom you may not need.

There's nothing inherently wrong with a wealth manager charging a load, but there is something inherently wrong with an investor thinking the wealth management advice they get is somehow free just because they didn't write the manager a check. A payment subtracted automatically out of your account's return without your seeing it explicitly identified is still money out of your pocket. A load fee may seem worthwhile if you have no idea where to start on your own with an active approach, but remember that the passive approach doesn't require the same amount of research, allowing you to pick a simple collection of index funds instead. (Index funds are far less likely to be sold with loads.)

In the 1980s and '90s, these kinds of commissions (some straightforward, some "hidden") were the main way wealth managers got paid, and it was the traditional stockbroker model: investors had to pay commissions on each trade. That approach still exists, especially at traditional full-service stock brokerage firms like Morgan Stanley or Merrill Lynch, but the approach has shifted significantly over time toward paying a percentage of assets.

In fact, paying a percentage of assets has become the dominant means by which consumers pay their wealth managers. The investment industry claims that this model is more neutral in terms of pushing products, based on the logic that if you pay the same basic fee no matter what investments are in your portfolio, the wealth manager has no incentive to sell you more expensive strategies.

I find this logic to be a self-serving rationalization, however, because even though they're receiving a flat percentage of assets, many wealth managers still want to be perceived by their clients as adding value by picking the active asset managers they claim will outperform. In these scenarios, paying a percentage of assets can either be expensive or a bargain, depending on the services provided and the fee rate.

Finally, a few wealth managers work on a retainer or hourly basis. Though uncommon, this approach can prove to be a good deal for certain consumers, since the service provided is clearly allocated to the time the wealth manager spends, the same way it would be for an attorney, tax accountant, or even a plumber. At least these fees are easy to understand.

Asset Management Fees

The vast majority of the time, asset managers get paid a percentage of the assets they manage, and sometimes they charge an extra amount tied to how well they perform. Asset management fees range from very low-cost offerings like indexing to others that are quite expensive.

But why would you pay asset managers widely different fees for investments in the same asset class? The answer depends on the common assumption that the higher the fee, the higher the returns your asset manager will earn you. Basically, you're betting in advance on an asset manager's ability to outperform the market. (Spoiler alert: Higher fees correlate with *worse* performance.)[26]

That false assumption brings us back to the active versus passive debate, as your choices around that will drive the asset management fees you pay since indexing costs so much less than active management.

While we'll wait until the next chapter for the research on why indexing has proven so effective for consumers (and so harmful to the investment industry's profits), we can now at least define how indexing works and why its cost structure makes it so appealing. Focusing for now on the US stock market, indexing basically means owning shares of every stock in an index.

One of the most well-known indexes is the Standard & Poor's 500, more commonly referred to as the S&P 500. It represents the stocks of five hundred large US companies, which makes it a *large-cap* index, meaning it includes mainly large companies as measured by total market capitalization. In contrast, a *small-cap* index includes mainly smaller companies. For example, the Russell 2000 is a small-cap index measuring the performance of the two thousand smaller companies included in the much broader Russell 3000, which covers almost the entire US stock market. All three of these indexes, and many others, are easily available through very low-cost index funds, which means the lowest possible asset management fees.

And while indexing offers a number of advantages over active management, the low fees provide the biggest benefit. According to Morningstar, the average fee for actively managed US equity funds in 2019 was 0.68 percent, more than seven times more expensive than the average fee for indexed funds, 0.09 percent.[27] That means that for a $100,000 portfolio, you'd pay $680 per year for active versus $90 per year for indexing.

Why do active managers charge so much more to their consumers? Since they're trying to beat the market with stock picking rather than just providing access to the whole market through indexing, they have to pay for expensive analysts and researchers to select the stocks they claim will perform the best. That's the argument anyway.

And it's an appealing argument, except for the historical results. The fact is active managers as a group can't make up enough in returns to offset their higher fees, meaning that investors are, on average and across time, worse off with active management compared to passive. For example, from 2004 to 2019, the average US stock mutual fund (including index and active) returned only 7.86 percent versus the US stock market returning 8.79 percent, a performance gap of nearly 1 percent per year.[28] In other words, the market itself performed a lot better than the average mutual fund, and the evidence shows that the high fees of active management are a major cause of that shortfall.

Indexing simply offers a much lower-cost alternative, with fees in the 0.05 percent to 0.15 percent range for most broad, diversified stock indexes. As we'll see later, these savings can really add up and compound over time.

Fees Can Be Hard to Spot

Naturally, any industry benefits if its clients don't fully understand how they're paying for something, since that lack of understanding makes it easier to slip high fees right past them. Some industries provide clear and easily understood pricing, like grocery stores and restaurants. Others, like the healthcare industry, have justifiably earned a bad reputation for making pricing notoriously complicated and difficult to understand.

Because of disclosure regulations, many investments do offer fairly straightforward information about costs. However, there are still a number of areas where investors don't find it easy to determine what they're really paying. In a survey of investors published in 2018, 37 percent of 401(k) participants mistakenly believed they didn't pay any fees, with another 22 percent unsure if they did.[29]

I encountered a simple example of how fees can be hidden

from the consumer while doing volunteer tax returns for low-income people. I chatted with a nice young woman about her job at a small insurance agency. She mentioned that in addition to selling insurance, her office offered investment advice to its customers. She proudly shared that they offered the service for free.

I knew that didn't sound right, for two reasons. First, investment advice is rarely free. Second, having worked with mutual funds as Morningstar's first research director, I knew of a type of load fund called B shares, where a chunk of the portfolio gets carved out for the first five years to pay the advisor—in this case, the insurance agent. I respectfully asked the woman if they were selling load mutual funds where the investors pay what's typically an extra 1 percent in fees per year for five years on top of the regular fee rate.

She confirmed that her office did, in fact, get paid that way. So was she lying when she said her firm provided free investment advice? Not exactly. In her mind, the fact that clients weren't specifically writing checks to her office meant they weren't actually paying for the advice for which funds to buy. But they *were* paying for it—just out of their returns rather than directly. Either way, the clients ended up with less wealth.

Incidentally, just so you understand how federal law treats her claim, the US Securities and Exchange Commission (SEC) would define her statement as lying if she'd made it in a sales context. Rather than her being intentionally dishonest, however, I suspect the woman's perspective represents a common misunderstanding. Members of my own family have assured me that when they visited a bank branch to learn about investment choices, they were offered options to get into investments without paying a fee or commission, when in fact they were offered the same load mutual fund that my volunteer friend's firm was offering their clients.

These stories illustrate just how dangerous the word "free" can be when you're looking at investment choices. You'll become a better consumer if you get into the habit of wondering how people offering "free" services like this get paid.

Part of consumers' attraction to the investment industry lies in how they presume, incorrectly, that because they're not paying cash up front, they're not paying extra fees. Load mutual funds intentionally make their fees less clear, similar to how paying points on a mortgage means you still pay a fee to a mortgage broker, but it gets embedded in the loan payments in a way that conveniently makes it harder to understand the exact costs.

For any payments based on a percentage of assets, including mutual fund load fees, the fees get deducted directly from an account, meaning you don't see what you're paying unless you look closely. Psychologically, this can make a difference. I've encountered consumers who balk at writing a check for $2,000 for a retainer but remain perfectly content to pay $12,000 in fees as a percentage of assets because it's hidden away such that they don't fully understand that's how the process works.

To further illustrate the dangers of hidden costs, let's take a brief look at a story involving an investment product that typically only applies to the very wealthy. This complicated product is called a *variable pre-paid forward* (VPPF), and it's effectively a combination of a loan, the purchase of a put option on a particular stock, and the sale of a call option on that same stock. A VPPF is typically used by someone who holds a large position in a single stock, often referred to in the investment business as holding a *concentrated position*. For the purpose of the story, it's not important to understand these complex terms or financial instruments, although it does illustrate how complexity can easily be used to hide away extra costs.

In our story, there was a wealthy investor who was receiving advice from the wealth management division of a big investment bank, which we'll call Advisor #1. This investor held $60 million of a concentrated position in a single stock that he wanted to diversify. So Advisor #1 got a quote from their trading desk for a $60 million VPPF and suggested to the client that he go ahead and enter into the contract.

The investor in this story, unlike many investors, knew he needed to get a second opinion on the contract pricing. So he took the offer from the bank to another firm that works in the world of VPPFs (we'll call this firm Advisor #2). Advisor #2 then went to the trading desks at five different investment banks, with the exact same specifications, to shop around for the best price without disclosing the end client. These banks also all knew that Advisor #2 was a savvy expert whom they couldn't easily bamboozle—to secure the contract, they had to offer their best price.

Lo and behold, when the five offers came in, the best one showed a full 2 percent savings on the original amount of $60 million. That's *$1.2 million* cheaper than the original offer. And the savings came from a reduction in hidden costs.

This outcome might prove shocking enough until the real punch line emerges: the trading desk that offered the rate that would save our investor $1.2 million came from *the same bank* that had made the original offer through Advisor #1.

Why? Well, the first time around, the bank probably figured their client wouldn't be sophisticated enough to understand fair pricing (not a bad assumption for an investment this complicated). But when they had to offer their best rate without knowing the end client, the huge markup they originally thought they could get away with wouldn't fly with the sophisticated Advisor #2, so they offered a much better price.

As with load mutual funds, there's nothing inherently unethical about a VPPF other than it presents a great opportunity to hide the actual cost to the investor.

Our last example of hidden fees comes to us from the world of *defined contribution* (DC) plans, a type of retirement plan. Across my nearly forty years working in the finance industry, I've seen a lot of different techniques used to bury fees so investors don't understand them. The retirement plan world offers some of the most egregious examples.

DC plans, including the 401(k), 403(b), and 457 plans, are named for the sections of the IRS code that address them, since they're all tax-deferred vehicles. However, unlike with taxable investments, employees often don't have any choice in the cost of the plan they're offered. They can generally pick from an assortment of available investments, but they don't have a choice as to what fees they pay out of their retirement savings.

The vast majority of DC plans offer mutual funds to their participants because these funds provide a convenient way for employees to own small balances in well-diversified portfolios. Then, in addition to the typical fees paid to the asset managers through the mutual funds, DC plans sometimes charge extra for administrative costs (like governmental filings), and the cost to pay the plan's wealth advisor for picking the mutual funds that are offered to employees.

Sometimes the employer pays these extra costs, but often—especially with smaller plans—the employees end up paying them through higher fees than they'd normally pay for the same taxable mutual funds (similar to a load).

For example, I once looked at a range of funds for a DC plan offered by what I consider a relatively ethical investment firm. The funds they offered were effectively the same as the load funds described earlier, in which an ongoing extra percentage of the assets go toward compensating a wealth manager. What boggled my mind when looking at this was the fact that, for each mutual fund, there were *seven different price rates* that an advisor could choose to charge the employee. The wealth manager and the employer got to pick which rate the employee paid based on how much the manager charged for their supposed expertise of picking the funds.

While these wealth managers would, of course, argue that they should be compensated for their work, the question remains as to whether their work actually adds value. Furthermore, in plans that have to pay high fees to wealth managers or cover administrative costs, the cheapest funds often aren't offered to the employees because they don't provide enough fee revenue to pay all those extra advisors. This means that investment managers are incentivized to choose the funds that provide the most profit for their bottom line, not the ones that most benefit the investors. They then get to dictate which options the employees can choose from to begin with.

DC fees remain among the most opaque, and it may prove challenging for you to find out about the fees you pay for them. These plans also display an incredibly wide range of fees, with some excellent, low-fee plans on the one hand and plenty of expensive offerings that gouge the employees on the other. For the investment industry, complicated and poorly understood pricing provides an excellent opportunity to charge too much for managing the retirement plans for millions of American workers.

Practical Tips on Controlling Fees

As a consumer, you face two major challenges when trying to figure out the right amount of fees to pay to have your money managed. The first is figuring out what services you want to buy, including whether to pay extra for active; the second is understanding what you're paying for so you can avoid getting taken for a ride. Your total wealth and peace of mind will improve from staying informed and on top of the fees you pay. Just as the influence of your brain's wiring gets de-emphasized compared to how to time or beat the market, the math for measuring the fees you pay often gets short shrift in the standard advice given for the best way to focus your investment research.

When it comes down to deciding how much to pay in fees, the main driver should be what services you need. If you're an investor who believes in active management and you think you're likely to find a wealth advisor who can add value by picking the managers who will outperform, then you believe that higher fees are justified by likely performance. If, like many investors, you're skeptical of asset managers' ability to outperform consistently, then you're also skeptical that wealth managers can identify in advance the asset managers who will do so. (For you skeptics, there remain a lot of services you still may need, like financial planning. We'll explore these in chapter 8.)

This is why every investor should, at the very least, add up all the costs for both categories of manager and compare that to what services they believe they actually need. To do this, first look carefully at all the layers of fees, calculating (or asking to have calculated) the costs for both wealth and asset management services. The total level of fees may also depend on the size of an investor's portfolio, since large portfolios can mean economies of scale for advisors.

The total fees are almost always shown as a percentage of your portfolio, say 0.75 percent in total fees for both wealth and asset management. Most individuals think in terms of actual dollars instead of percentages when they buy something—if we have to pay for a new roof, we generally don't think of it as a percentage of the value of our house, for example. But percentages are standard for the investment industry. Though it may not be intuitive, the only way to know if the fees you're paying are reasonable or a rip-off is to compare the percentages across various choices and then convert those percentages into actual dollars.

As you do this, keep in mind how complexity and the appearance of activity both help the investment industry sell you more expensive strategies while persuading you that you'll be earning a higher return in exchange, a false promise on average. This is why controlling fees comes down to deciding which services you want to buy, with the knowledge that passive investing has much lower fees than active.

Moving beyond the choice between active and passive, consumers also face the challenge of knowing exactly what they're paying for—that is, getting the kind of advice they need for specific situations, rather than the ongoing management of a portfolio. The investment industry focuses heavily on the latter, often implying that the best portfolios (active) require a lot of monitoring (not true for indexing).

So what about clients who don't need fancy ongoing portfolio management but do have specific questions about their financial situation? Questions like:

- Am I saving enough to fund my retirement?
- Should I withdraw assets first from my 401(k), my Roth IRA, or my taxable accounts?
- Since I'm receiving an inheritance next year, should I adjust my own asset allocation to reflect the additional assets?
- How should I think of my pension payments in the context of my portfolio?

All these questions are valid and may benefit from expert advice. Unfortunately, the investment industry doesn't usually offer the opportunity to get such questions answered without including the entire (expensive) managing of a portfolio. Hourly billing offers a great way to get questions like this answered, but this payment method remains rare since it tends to be much less lucrative for wealth advisors than getting paid to manage portfolios.

The bottom line is it's important to understand exactly

what you're paying for and exactly what you pay. Whether it's $2,000 or $20,000 or $200,000 in fees, it's money coming out of your pocket. One technique is to sit down once a year and write a hypothetical check for the total amount of fees you're paying. This makes what you pay more concrete than an abstract percentage.

Are High Fees Ever Justified?

What's the "right" fee rate for an investor to pay? Unfortunately, this is a nuanced question that doesn't lead to clear advice across the board, as each individual's situation is different. However, the history of how the investment industry has performed over many decades does provide guidance on where it might be worthwhile to pay higher fees versus where fees unnecessarily enrich either wealth or asset managers and not you, the investor.

If the question is whether paying higher fees earns higher performance, then, as we've seen, the answer for most asset classes becomes much clearer: somewhere between rarely and never. In a 2010 Morningstar report on fees, Russell Kinnel put it beautifully: "If there's anything in the whole world of mutual funds that you can take to the bank, it's that expense ratios help you make a better decision. In every single time period and data point tested, low-cost funds beat high-cost funds."[30]

Chapter 6

The Industry's Track Record

NOW THAT WE'VE LOOKED at the biases of investment managers and how they get paid, let's look at how effectively—or ineffectively—they're managing their clients' money.

We've seen how much our emotions dominate our financial behavior, including our tendency to choose the Chocolate Cake (the sexy math of traditional stock picking) over the Broccoli. However, some boring math is critically important, specifically the industry's track record, which provides powerful evidence that active management has led to lower returns on average.

Investment managers face a strong incentive to pander to your cravings for someone who can peer into a crystal ball and soothe you by foretelling the future. Unfortunately, the research shows how investment managers like me have been proven to be pretty lame at using a crystal ball to either successfully time the market (*asset allocation*) or pick the individual stocks that will outperform (*security selection*).

We're about to look at both versions of a crystal ball—and their actual track records—in more detail, but first, we need a brief overview of asset allocation and security selection.

Asset Allocation (Timing the Market) versus Security Selection (Picking the Stocks)

There are two essential levels in investing: asset allocation and security selection. Asset allocation is the mix of broad asset classes in a portfolio, like how much in stocks and how much in bonds; security selection is the act of choosing the individual securities within an asset class, e.g., which stocks or bonds.

This means that once you (or your wealth manager) have picked your asset allocation, you then need to decide how to implement each asset class through security selection (what kind of asset manager to hire).

At both levels you face a choice of active versus passive. With active asset allocation, you're putting faith in your (or your wealth manager's) ability to time the market, i.e., shift toward risky assets like stocks when they're going to do well and toward safer assets like bonds when the risky investments are going to do poorly. With active security selection, you (or your wealth manager) put faith in an asset manager's ability to beat the market by picking the individual securities, like stocks, that will do better on average than others.

The table below summarizes the choices.

Table 6. Active vs. Passive Asset Allocation and Security Selection

	Active Asset Allocation	Passive Asset Allocation
Active Security Selection	You time the market, adjusting your proportion of stocks, for example, based on whether you think stocks will outperform or underperform bonds. You either pick your own stocks or hire an active stock manager.	You keep your proportion of stocks constant and don't forecast whether you think stocks will outperform or underperform bonds. You either pick your own stocks or hire an active stock manager.
Passive Security Selection	You time the market, adjusting your weighting of stocks, for example, based on whether you think stocks will outperform or underperform bonds. For the choice of which stocks, you index.	You keep your weighting of stocks constant and don't forecast whether you think stocks will outperform or underperform bonds. For the choice of which stocks, you index.

For security selection to outperform, it must consistently beat a market benchmark. For an asset allocation to outperform, it must beat the static proportion in each asset class.

In both asset allocation and security selection, your brain's wiring leads you to crave the control and potential success of the active approach. Unfortunately, the research overwhelmingly proves that a passive approach at both levels has consistently made investors wealthier.

Crystal Ball #1: Picking Which Stocks Will Outperform

Now, it's true that some active asset managers do outperform, typically around 20 percent. But that means 80 percent of active asset managers fail to beat their benchmarks, usually by significant margins. Based on the research, I use a rule of thumb that, on average, active management underperforms by about 1 percent per year of lost return. This means that if you have a portfolio of $100,000, you'll be less wealthy by $1,000 per year. While that may sound trivial, it really adds up when compounded over time.

I mentioned this statistic earlier, but it's worth highlighting again: from 2004 to 2019, the entire US stock market earned an average annual return of 8.79 percent, while the average US stock mutual fund earned 7.86 percent, highlighting the lower returns caused by higher fees.[31] In case you think it's just retail mutual funds that trail the market, the evidence looks pretty much the same for big institutional investors like public pension funds.[32]

How could all the active managers fail to beat the market? Are they just not very smart? On the contrary: too many active managers are too smart. This means that even though they charge top dollar for their services, the bar is raised too high for them to earn enough to offset their fees. If they were to charge no fees, then active would likely provide closer to the same returns as passive investing (although the extra trading can harm returns too). The higher fees are the main reason active managers underperform. Thus, they're not stupid, just too expensive.

So let's go with the research and assume that 80 percent of active asset managers will underperform their benchmarks. Why not just find the ones in the 20 percent that outperform? Well, because the asset managers who do outperform don't do it consistently.

In other words, you can pick the asset managers who have outperformed historically, but there's no guarantee they'll continue to do so—in fact, the numbers show it's unlikely they will. Of course, this doesn't keep wealth managers from trying to persuade you that even though the industry as a whole has failed to beat the market, they provide such sophisticated analysis that they can pick the active asset managers who will outperform, a pitch you should view with skepticism.

Why do we bring such confidence to our own abilities to pick the stocks that will outperform or project that predictive ability onto others? Part of it goes back to the human brain. Our brains have evolved to be great at identifying patterns—another skill that helped us survive as a species hundreds of thousands of years ago. But while pattern recognition might have provided an advantage in hunting migrating game, for example, today, our inclination to spot patterns means we often see them even when they don't exist. As investment researcher Jeff Sommer puts it, "Short-term financial news often amounts to little more than meaningless 'noise,'" and investors then "try to make sense out of this noise, and to no avail."[33]

In fairness to active asset managers, it's too extreme a position to say that active is always awful. Nonetheless, the data show that active stock management has destroyed value for investors on average, over time. (In fact, while Aperio Group has offered some active strategies for investors who wanted to make certain types of bets, we still didn't claim we'd outperform before taxes. We suggested that some form of indexing is the best overall approach.)

If it sounds as though active couldn't be that bad, you might think of it from another angle, one described very effectively by Larry Swedroe in his excellent book *Think, Act, and Invest Like Warren Buffett*. Swedroe explains that the combination of all active and passive investors, by definition, has to add up to the total stock market, whatever the breakdown between the two.[34]

Since passive investors, by definition, earn the market return before expenses (management fees, trading costs, and administration), this means active investors must earn the market return before expenses too, since every stock has to be owned by someone.

Here comes the moment of truth: when you add in all the expenses, active costs a lot more on average than passive, thus proving that even without researching historical returns, we can safely state that the returns of all active investors after expenses will be less than the returns of all passive investors. This absolute truth tends to horrify active asset managers when I point it out.

Crystal Ball #2: Market Timing

Unfortunately for fans of active management, and for wealth managers who promise results based on their skill with a crystal ball, the data on market timing (i.e., active asset allocation) disappoint just as much as the data on active security selection.

In this case, the evidence often comes from institutional investors (companies or organizations that invest on behalf of other people), like pension funds. In a research paper on market timing in multi-asset class mutual funds, Andrew Clare stated, "Timing skill is rare and is found among a small minority of funds."[35]

Pension consultant firm Ennis Knupp reflected this reality years ago, while they were still an independent company, saying that "few investment strategies have been debunked—by academics and practitioners alike—as roundly as has market timing."[36]

Charles Ellis, an early proponent of passive investing, also said, "Market timing is a truly wicked idea. Don't try it."[37]

Of course, as with security selection, there have been examples of successful market timing.[38] However, also like security selection, the odds remain stacked against you as an investor if you operate like you or someone you hire can rely on a crystal ball. Whereas many wealth managers claim an ability to pick the asset managers who will beat the market through security selection, in my experience, they tend to tout less often their own skills at market timing. At least with market timing there seems to be more honesty about how hard it is to predict market movements with any consistency.

This more honest approach may not prevent wealth advisors from implying that, during a rough storm, you're better off with their firm hand on the tiller, however. Soothing a panicked investor during a market collapse can provide a lot of value in terms of encouraging better behavior, but implying superior skill at navigating rough waters in terms of knowing when to shift asset allocation (a technique sometimes called *risk on/risk off*) slides into reliance on a crystal ball.

Advisor and author Rick Ferri compiled some helpful summaries of the dismal failure among both professionals and individuals when they try to time the market. He cites, among other evidence, the poor track record of public allocations from Wall Street firms versus a static allocation, as well as the ineffective predictions of market timing newsletters. Turning to the record of individuals, he points to inflows and outflows of risky assets that follow the pattern of reflecting whatever just happened, like reducing stock exposure right after a market drop. Ferri found no evidence of individuals' ability on average to accurately forecast market changes.[39]

Similarly, a Morningstar study of market timing by mutual

funds found that from 2003 to 2018, the average tactical-allocation fund (active) returned 3.4 percent per year, while the static (passive, or no market timing) Vanguard Balanced Index with the same overall risk returned 6.6 percent, a whopping victory for passive asset allocation.[40]

Past Success Doesn't Guarantee Future Success

When investing in stocks, it sounds so sensible to pick the active strategies that will supposedly beat the market average. After all, who wouldn't want to perform better than average? But the math tells us the opposite story: choosing indexing isn't settling for average, it's settling for *the top 10 percent or 20 percent* when compared to active, depending on the research you select.

Though the data so strongly support indexing, this choice presents a challenge to how our brains are wired. Our brains' craving for control, even if illusory, means it can be upsetting to acknowledge that financial markets are, in fact, random and unpredictable.

The fickle nature of markets means that how you measure active managers matters a great deal. I've often encountered investment consultants who don't manage your money but instead simply suggest active managers. They might provide recommendations for, say, three active managers for stocks based on their research. For the do-it-yourself (DIY) investor, this may seem like a worthwhile one-time expense.

Unfortunately, their research is subject to the same biases and blind spots as any other industry professional. While they may justify their recommendations based on those active managers' recent outperformance, as a general rule, they don't keep track of their *own* success in *choosing* these managers, which is the first thing any investor should ask them about.

In other words, the question shouldn't be, "Which active stock managers have beaten the market recently?" Finding the few managers with successful records is easy.

Instead, the question should be, "What's your track record for choosing active stock managers who have continued to beat the market after you've recommended them?" Investment consultants who recommend active managers want you to believe that managers' past success means they'll continue to succeed in the future—even though the data conclusively show this isn't reliably the case.

The Predicament of Prediction

It's also easy to fall victim to another psychological bias when looking at stock market valuations: misreading what a hot business trend actually means for your portfolio's returns. For example, in the late 1990s, whenever I would talk about indexing, many investors would respond skeptically, saying,

"Don't you realize that the Internet is going to change the world's economy?"

They meant that if they took my advice and invested using indexing, they'd somehow miss out on the upside of sweeping changes in the economy. But this conclusion ignored the fact that investors had already bid up the prices on Internet companies to reflect the coming change. Therefore, since the market had already "priced in" the effect of the Internet's changes, an index fund would capture those returns without resorting to trying to pick the individual stocks or industries.

The question investors and investment managers should've been asking wasn't, "Will the economy be changed by the Internet?" but "Am I more accurate than the entire stock market at determining how much I should pay for Internet stocks given that the Internet will change the economy?" That's a very different question, and the research shows that the vast majority of us, whether professionals or amateurs, don't possess superior skill at predicting which industries or stocks appear over- or undervalued.

Here's another example. In 2020, I was advising a friend on her portfolio, and she was very open to the idea of using indexing as her main exposure to owning stocks. However, she held one mutual fund that focused on the healthcare industry. When I asked about this, she said a friend of hers had recommended that concentration. Her friend's logic reflected the assumption that as the population of the United States ages, healthcare will become more important as an industry, meaning it would be smart to overweight her holdings of healthcare companies.

Just like in the earlier example of the Internet frenzy of the late 1990s, however, the question shouldn't have been, "Will healthcare become an increasingly important part of the economy?" but "Am I more accurate than the entire stock market at predicting the performance of healthcare stocks given that industry's increasing dominance?"

Predicting which industry will grow the fastest isn't all that hard; predicting which industry will provide better stock returns has been proven to be fruitless. To put it another way, any single company (or industry), no matter how exciting its prospects, can still be overpriced when it comes to its stock (or collective stocks).

How to Spot the Industry's Glaring Conflict of Interest

The debate remains vibrant as to whether the few managers who outperform do so consistently enough to make any active investing worthwhile. However, there is no real debate, vibrant or otherwise, about the fact that active management in its entirety has destroyed value for investors. When the industry tries to sell active management, it tends to cite the exceptions, but almost never admits that the odds are stacked against you when you try to beat the market. Why do they avoid that unwelcomed truth?

Most of the motivation to support active comes not from unbiased academic research, but from a self-serving industry that can make a lot more money by claiming skills with a crystal ball. I'm continually flabbergasted at how much the financial press ignores the conclusive historical performance data when reporting on the best strategies or the entire active–passive debate.

But of course the financial press has an incentive to get you excited about chocolate cake: broccoli isn't scrumptious clickbait. It's unlikely you'll ever see a headline like "Here Are the Investments You Need to Own in Today's Market: The Same Boring Index Strategies We Told You about Last Year and the Year Before." (You can sense how misleading I find most marketing. At my firm, the staff joked that if I were in charge of marketing for a fancy sushi restaurant, I'd come up with the tagline "Hey, you want to buy some cold, dead fish?")

Both the financial press and the investment industry can offer great insights, as we'll explore in chapter 8. However, don't take investment experts at face value when they defend active strategies, as they have strong incentive to claim they have nonexistent predictive skills. They're afraid that if they admit they can't predict much of anything, you might think you don't need to hire them. And this is a valid worry in some cases, as many investors don't need a wealth manager.

To further show the industry's bias against passive investing, many critics point out that if everyone indexed, the stock market wouldn't get priced effectively and the whole system would collapse. This does raise a valid point: active management, in some form, is essential to keeping what's called *price discovery* working properly. For the stock market to function efficiently, the prices of stocks need to get adjusted constantly to reflect the changing prospects for individual companies or the overall economy.

However, indexing critics usually leave out any real analysis as to how much of the stock market could be indexed before price discovery might be endangered. Ironically, if you're a supporter of active stock picking, you should *welcome* indexing becoming so dominant that price discovery doesn't work as well as it should, since that would mean more promising opportunities for active to outperform.

Another line I keep hearing from the investment industry reflects the assumption that active stock picking works better than passive in down markets. I've read this claim many times, but I've never seen any evidence to prove it over longer time periods like ten years or more. In fact, the research[41] shows that active fails just as much in down markets as in up markets, but that doesn't prevent the self-serving view that while active may not work all the time, it can help you more when you're anxious. The industry might as well say, "While our ability to pick stocks in down markets has historically been no better than in up markets, we can prey on your fears more effectively during a down market since that's when you're even more desperate for the illusion of control."

While investment pros who want to sell you on active may resist acknowledging the data on the industry's poor overall track record, the disturbing truth for them is how very smart and reliably prudent indexing has proven to be. At the very least, pay close attention to the economic incentives of anyone trying to give you advice. (Think how much more money I could make selling you something I know you crave, even though the research strongly indicates it's bad for your financial health.)

This is why focusing on fees is important. Remember, fees are the number-one factor you can control, and though, like broccoli, they might sound boring, low fees do provide for a very healthy portfolio.

To Index or Not to Index?

Even the staunchest supporters of indexing must acknowledge that in spite of the evidence of active management's failure on average over time, rigidly dismissing all active isn't warranted. I've spoken with investors who take 90 percent of their stock allocation and put it in indexing, but then try to beat the market with the remaining 10 percent. Even an indexing evangelical like me finds that a perfectly tame approach, since the limited scope of the active means it can't do much harm, but it still allows the fun of trying to beat the market.

I'm not arguing that you're foolish to do anything but index. Instead, I'm pushing you to raise the bar high, switching from thinking you need to hire a wealth manager who will then pick the best active asset managers to thinking that your default should be to index because it's so low cost, tax efficient, and reliable.

With indexing you do run the risk of not making it into the very narrow group of active managers who may actually beat the market, but with active, you run the risk of finishing at the bottom of the heap. In other words, it's foolish to take the risk of achieving that slight chance of the top 10 or 20 percent of performers rather than locking in performing at the 80th or 90th percentile. Why gamble on the slim odds of outperforming when it risks performing terribly?

When we discussed how the brains of investment managers work, we focused on how their incentives lead to cognitive dissonance ("I know active usually doesn't work, but my choice of active has nothing to do with my own compensation being higher") and confirmation bias ("I know the vast majority of research shows that active has destroyed value, but here's one article that says otherwise for certain situations"). This means that, unfortunately, in many cases you'll be the only one truly looking out for your own interests.

Now that you understand the motivation, compensation, and track record of the industry that's trying so hard to sell you its services, you can be wary of the sales pitches from wizards with a crystal ball—but be careful not to become so cynical that you ignore the real value wealth managers can provide. To learn how to achieve a healthy balance, we'll now take everything we've learned and turn to how to go about implementing a great portfolio, whether on your own or by hiring a professional.

Part III

HOW TO INVEST

Chapter 7

Index Investing

SO YOUR OWN BRAIN WORKS against you and the industry incentivizes wishful thinking. At this point, you may be ready to give up on investing altogether in favor of stuffing your cash under your mattress. Don't worry! Now we're going to look at how to avoid these pitfalls by picking the best indexing strategies for your portfolio, focusing on simple being the best default.

The Broadly Diversified Passive Approach

As a consumer, you face a bewildering variety across the many thousands of index funds available, each based on an equally bewildering range of benchmarks. *Benchmarks* are the standard against which the performance of a security or mutual fund (or an active asset manager) can be compared—they're indexes created across all types of asset classes, like the S&P 500 and the Dow Jones Industrial Average. For stocks, a benchmark is an equity index that a portfolio gets compared against.

As you approach the virtual shelves crowded with so many choices, keep in mind that there are two different senses of the term *index investing*:

1. The *technical* sense of owning a portfolio that tracks a benchmark without trying to outperform it.
2. The *ownership* sense of holding most or all of an entire asset class, like stocks, through an index fund.

For example, if, as a US investor, you have an entire portfolio consisting of one index fund that holds a wide variety of industries but stocks from only Thailand, technically you're indexed in your approach (meaning #1). However, that narrow choice provides a ghastly lack of diversification given how much of the world's stock markets you've elected to ignore.

Narrow indexes for one part of the world's stock market can capture just one country, industry, or type of stocks (say, small-cap companies). These narrower choices offer excellent features for specific situations in complicated portfolios in which you want to overweight a certain area or fill a gap—for example, by taking an existing US stock portfolio that holds only large-cap companies and adding small-cap stocks. Most investors don't need the narrower versions, however—think back to all the evidence against trying to predict what will outperform the market, be it individual stocks, specific industries, or geographical regions.

So, for our purposes, indexing is *diversified* passive investing. This means that most of the time you'll want to focus on the broadest, most inclusive benchmarks available. For an example of meaning #2, if you own the entire US stock market through one fund, then you own the biggest stock market in the world, and you don't have to worry about overweighting or underweighting the stocks of small companies, large companies, or certain industries. You can also invest in one single benchmark for the entire global stock market, which I call simply investing in capitalism, since you're buying stocks around the globe in the same proportions as all the world's investors combined.

For the purposes of this book, when we talk about indexing, we'll really be focusing on what we'll call *broadly diversified passive* (BDP) stock investing, which delivers an entire asset class at very low cost. You can build a BDP portfolio yourself or hire a wealth manager to do so on your behalf as long as they're focused on low fees for the asset managers they select for you.

Understanding How Weighting Schemes Work

To understand how stock indexes are constructed, we'll first need to focus on their "weighting schemes," or how the percentage of each stock in an index gets set. The most common method for this weights stocks by market capitalization (market "cap" for short), i.e., the total value of a company's stock.

For example, if Microsoft has 7.6 billion shares held by investors at $203 per share, that makes a total market capitalization of $1,543 billion, or $1.5 trillion. If we wanted to find Microsoft's weight in an index, say the S&P 500, we would then add up the market cap of all 500 stocks to get about $27 trillion. Dividing $1.5 trillion by $27 trillion, we find that Microsoft's weight in the S&P 500 is 5.72 percent.[42]

This makes the S&P 500 a cap-weighted index because the percentage of every stock in the index is based on the proportion of the stock's market capitalization to the total capitalization of the entire index.[43]

Cap-weighted indexes offer two advantages. First, they automatically readjust to price changes. Say, for example, that Microsoft announces positive news that makes its stock price rise by 5 percent while the rest of the market remains unchanged. This would mean that Microsoft's weight in the index would go up too, and your investment in the index fund would automatically adjust along with it, without any stocks needing to be bought or sold. A cap-weighted portfolio requires only minimal rebalancing most of the time, keeping it both effective and simple.

Second, since a cap-weighted index reflects the entire stock market's opinion, it's the purest form of indexing, since the market as a whole sets the pricing. This is why I consider cap-weighted indexes the only true measure of the entire market and thus the best choice for benchmarks. I would define anything that's not cap-weighted as an active strategy. This doesn't mean that anything other than cap-weighted indexes should be avoided, but cap-weighted benchmarks and index funds tied to those benchmarks do offer the best place to start with the broadly diversified passive approach.

Which Benchmark Is Best?

Both active and passive managers have benchmarks. However, with a pure index strategy, the benchmark, the index, and the fund or portfolio should effectively all show the same performance after adjusting for fees. (Unlike an active strategy, which tries to outperform the benchmark.)

With indexing now so popular, all the well-known indexes are available through mutual funds or individual accounts managed just for one investor. As it turns out, though, the most famous aren't necessarily the best choice. In fact, many of these well-known benchmarks provide poor diversification and therefore make terrible choices for index investing, as you can see in this table.

Table 7. Comparison of Top Benchmarks

Index	Description	Analysis
Dow Jones Industrial Average	30 large US companies	Interesting from a historical perspective, but fairly useless. With just thirty stocks, it's silly that it remains the most widely quoted index in press coverage given how poorly it represents the US stock market. Worse, it's a price-weighted, not cap-weighted, index, unlike all the others in this list. In its favor, historical performance hasn't been all that different from the S&P 500 though.
S&P 500	500 mainly large-cap US companies picked by a committee	One of the most widely used indexes for US stocks. It provides decent exposure to the US market but leaves out most small companies. Stocks are selected by committee, which means it has an active component. Not a bad index, but not ideal.
NASDAQ Composite	Over 3,300 stocks listed on the NASDAQ exchange	Popular, but tech-heavy, benchmark often reported in news coverage. Given its narrow focus, it makes a poor choice for investors (except for rare and unusual circumstances) since it lacks optimal diversification across industries.

Russell 3000	Roughly the 3,000 largest US companies	A reliable index for almost the entire US stock market. An excellent choice for US exposure since it includes large, medium, and small US companies.
Russell 2000	The 2,000 smallest companies of the Russell 3000	An acceptable small-cap index, but only for the narrow goal of increasing small-cap exposure. Can be inefficient for taxable accounts since it has more turnover.
MSCI EAFE (Europe, Australasia, Far East)	900 large and mid-cap stocks from developed non-US markets	A widely used foreign stock benchmark that excludes Canada and emerging markets. Not the best for most investors who seek foreign stock exposure.
MSCI World	Global benchmark with over 1,500 large and mid-cap stocks from developed markets, including the US	Good benchmark for global developed markets (US and foreign), but excludes emerging markets. Also offered in versions that include small-cap or foreign only.
MSCI ACWI (All Country World Index)	Global benchmark with foreign and US, including emerging markets	Excellent global benchmark for large- and mid-cap stocks. Also offered in versions that include small-cap or foreign only.

When selecting benchmarks, investors often find it helpful to choose one from the list above since they're well known and recognized. I tend to recommend the broadest coverage possible. Thus, for the US stock market, the Russell 3000 (and others like it) represents an excellent index since it covers almost the entire market with a cap-weighted benchmark.

This kind of comprehensive benchmark offers an additional advantage in that you don't have to worry about the tax consequences of periodic resets. For example, Russell also offers a version of just large- and mid-cap stocks called the Russell 1000, leaving the remaining small-cap companies in the Russell 2000. Owning the Russell 2000, though, means you're vulnerable to tax consequences of companies that may have gotten large enough to move from the Russell 2000 to the Russell 1000 in one year.

There are also firms that trade around the periodic realignment of benchmarks, trying to benefit from knowing in advance which companies may be added or dropped. That problem goes away almost entirely when you invest in an index strategy based on a broad benchmark like the Russell 3000, because when you own large-, mid-, and small-cap companies all in the same vehicle, you don't have to worry about recalibrating. The same idea applies to global benchmarks like the MSCI ACWI, in which owning an indexed strategy based on that benchmark gets you everything you need for stock markets around the world.

This table shows some of the broadest-equity benchmarks, which are the best places to start.

Table 8. Broad-Equity Benchmarks.

Bench-mark	Geographic Coverage	Advan-tages	Disadvan-tages	Size of Companies Included
Russell 3000	United States	Most com-prehensive	None	Covers large, medium, and small compa-nies
MSCI ACWI	All major stock markets worldwide	Covers US, foreign devel-oped, and emerging markets based on global cap weighting	Ignores "home country bias," mean-ing over-weighting the country where you live	Covers large and medium companies, but also comes in a version called the ACWI IMI that in-cludes small
MSCI ACWI ex-US	All major non-US stock markets	Excellent single broad benchmark for foreign stocks	If you use this bench-mark, you have to pick how much you have in foreign stocks	Covers large and medium companies, but also comes in a version called ACWI ex-US IMI that in-cludes small

Should you pay extra for the value of a known benchmark? Because benchmark creation has become much easier with advances in technology, many low-cost index offerings now rely on generic or in-house benchmarks to avoid high benchmark vendor fees, which means that paying up for a name brand rarely proves justified, especially for broad-based, capitalization-weighted benchmarks. Paying more for a brand name index is just like paying more for a brand-name drug, when the generic version is often chemically identical.

For example, in 2012, Vanguard dropped MSCI as the provider of benchmarks for a number of its index funds in order to save on costs. They switched to a rather obscure academic database of benchmarks from the University of Chicago known as the Center for Research in Security Prices (CRSP). In this case, Vanguard was just trying to save money for its investors, and they'd done excellent research that showed it didn't make that much difference to move from a name brand like MSCI to CRSP.

Thus, just because you haven't heard of a benchmark doesn't mean it should be avoided. Most broad-coverage benchmarks rely on cap-weighting and remain quite reliable as a general rule.

Indexing Across Other Asset Classes

So far we've focused mainly on stock indexes. But what about bonds and cash assets? Does indexing offer the same benefits?

For bonds, the short answer is no. When looking for bond strategies, either through mutual funds or separately managed accounts (for those with bigger balances), fees by themselves act as the easiest way of assessing a bond portfolio. This means indexing doesn't matter the way it does with stocks.

Additionally, while bond index funds can be excellent diversification tools, they ignore fundamental decisions like your tax rate and whether you should hold municipal or taxable bonds. Thus, for bonds, unlike for stocks, your decision doesn't just boil down to active versus passive. Instead, it should start with your tax bracket and risk tolerance, as we'll discuss later, and then focus on low fees.

What about cash? Just like with bond strategies, the two keys to a good choice in the cash asset class are understanding how your tax bracket affects your after-tax return and then finding low fees (and of course risk still matters). In general, taxable investors with the highest tax rates usually earn higher after-tax returns with municipal money market funds, while lower-bracket taxable investors do better with taxable money market funds. Indexing doesn't really exist for money market funds, so once you've picked taxable or municipal, fees will dominate all other factors in choosing the best one.

Unnecessarily high fees matter enormously for money market funds. Unfortunately for investors, brokerage firms won't let you pick money market funds from other investment companies, as in most cases they make too much money from offering you only their own funds. In addition, you often earn a much lower rate on what's called a *sweep account* in a brokerage account where you own stocks or exchange-traded funds (ETFs). Sweep accounts may still be money market funds, but since they invest your cash automatically, you can earn significantly less than in money market accounts that you buy and sell yourself.

While money market funds have offered higher rates than high-yield cash accounts at banks for the vast majority of years since they were introduced in the 1970s, there have been times of unusual economic turmoil when money market funds have offered no return, like when they pay 0.01 percent, effectively zero. After the 2008 to 2009 financial crisis and the Federal Reserve's response to the pandemic in early 2020, certain banks offered higher rates than money market funds for a time. In such periods, you may be able to find a higher return at a bank, although if you're fortunate enough to have large cash balances, you should be careful of the FDIC insurance limit of $250,000 per account and avoid putting more than that amount in any one institution.

Passive Asset Allocation

As we discussed in the previous chapter, passive investing applies to both security selection (indexing versus active) and asset allocation (static versus active, when the latter is known as market timing).

My advice to avoid active doesn't mean you should ignore the fact that stocks have, on average and over time, earned significantly higher returns than cash, bonds, or even real estate. Paying attention to long-term return patterns makes sense in terms of your asset allocation. What doesn't make sense is trying to assess whether the stock market looks overvalued or undervalued at any particular moment in time and adjusting your asset allocation accordingly.

Periods of market upheaval and explosive volatility present a psychological challenge: remaining steadfast to a passive asset allocation. When people ask me about adjusting their asset allocation during a bad market period, I respond in one of two ways depending on whether the proposed change seems permanent or temporary.

Investors who may need to make a permanent change are likely learning that their risk tolerance isn't as high as they'd presumed during calmer times. In effect, therefore, they're saying that they need a permanently safer asset allocation given their own behavior, which I view as useful self-knowledge. Maybe they had an asset allocation of 80 percent risky and 20 percent safer, and they just can't stick with that much risk during frightening stock market drops. Although it would have been preferable to know this about their risk tolerance before opting for 80/20, in this case, I might recommend they stick with 60 percent risky and 40 percent safer moving forward.

But then we have the investors who tell me they prefer a safer asset allocation in the middle of a crisis, but they'll return to a more aggressive allocation once the market calms down and becomes less frothy, i.e., when the risk goes back down to "normal levels." Basically, they're telling me they want to engage in market timing (active asset allocation). As you know by now, though it may feel psychologically appealing, this strategy is as foolhardy as trying to pick the stocks that will outperform. In these cases, it's the investor's *perception* of risk that has jumped up significantly, not the potential risk itself (which, when measured over a long time horizon, doesn't change as much).

The stock market is always dangerous, and as an investor, you risk making bad investment decisions when you falsely interpret recent calm as a sign of future calm (or the opposite). Research has shown that we tend to base our expectations for the stock market on the behavior of the last six months, but we need to look at stock market behavior over many decades if we're long-term investors. This will help us nudge our brains toward a longer-term perspective than what our emotions push us toward. Otherwise, we succumb to fear and the illusion of control.

The Truth Victorious

While from its inception in 1999 Aperio has made the case for indexing, up until about 2012 I wouldn't have predicted the sea change in favor of stock indexing in the United States. Indexing has become common and widespread, growing from 13 percent of US equity mutual fund assets in 1998 to over 50 percent in 2019, according to *Institutional Investor*.[44]

Your perspective on this growth in popularity depends entirely on whether your loyalties lie with consumers or with the investment industry. Because of the crushing effect on low-ered revenue streams, the active management industry has been reeling since about 2010, as would any industry watching its income erode. Throughout the history of capitalism, many industries have gone through similar wrenching changes, and you might have more sympathy for some groups than for others.

For example, in the first half of the nineteenth century, a group of laborers in Britain were so threatened by automation in the weaving industry that they organized to destroy factories and equipment. For those workers, who called themselves Luddites, the change from industrialization meant horrific labor conditions and the mistreatment of workers. Today, "Luddite" has become a nickname for those who resist technological change.

Obviously, we should feel sympathy for anyone whose livelihood is threatened by economic change—even active managers. Nonetheless, the existential threat to its revenue doesn't justify the investment industry continuing to sell the efficacy of skills that are repeatedly proven false.

This is why it's been incredibly heartening for me to watch consumers wean themselves from the traditional pitch of active management and march with their dollars toward much lower-cost strategies. I'm naturally such a skeptic that it caught me off guard when the 2008 to 2009 financial meltdown caused enough investors to declare that they'd had enough with active management. The good news for investors is that many wealth managers have now been forced to include passive strategies, largely as a result of clients paying more attention to fees.

Many consumers have turned to broccoli after finally noticing the bad financial-health effects of too much chocolate cake.

The investment industry hasn't ignored this increased focus on fees. In fact, some asset management firms now offer indexing at only slightly above free, with expense ratios as low as 0.02 percent, which by historical standards is ridiculously cheap.

At this point, you might well ask, "I understand how indexing is a wiser bet than active management, but does it mean I shouldn't hire a wealth manager?" In the next chapter, I'll provide guidance on whether your own situation suggests you're better off doing it yourself or hiring a professional.

Chapter 8

Doing It Yourself versus Hiring a Professional

IN AN ICONIC SCENE from *The Wizard of Oz*, after Dorothy and her companions have successfully vanquished the Wicked Witch of the West, they return to the Wizard of Oz with the witch's broomstick as proof of their quest. Of course, the Wizard has just been posing as a magician, and Dorothy's dog, Toto, heroically unmasks the fraud, exposing the reality of a regular man standing behind a curtain, pulling levers and speaking into a microphone. Defensively, he calls out, "Pay no attention to the man behind the curtain," hoping that he can somehow continue to fool them.

When I think of how much of the investment industry tries to hide or justify its fees, in effect the line becomes for me, "Pay no attention to the fees behind the curtain." But although the industry often tries to obfuscate fees, the real metaphor for hiring investment managers ends up being more nuanced.

After Dorothy realizes they've been hoodwinked, she marches over to the Wizard and accuses him of being a bad man. He responds that he's actually a good man, but admits that he's a bad wizard. This is the nuance I see in the investment industry: it's when advisors pretend to have magical foresight that investors need to be wary of getting played.

But remember, even though he's been outed as a fraud as a wizard, the Wizard of Oz does provide supportive and helpful advice to the Scarecrow, the Tin Woodman, and the Cowardly Lion, all of whom benefit greatly from his counsel. Similarly, wealth managers can offer a lot of potentially useful services—as long as they avoid posturing by claiming they can foretell the future.

Useful Services

Let's start with the many valuable things an advisor can provide an investor. Each investor may or may not need every service, but when the need exists, the following can prove beneficial.

1. Financial Planning

For our purposes, financial planning is the cash-flow forecasting of your life, including how much you're saving, how much you can withdraw from a portfolio, and how much your portfolio is likely to grow. You can figure all this out by yourself, but it takes time and some understanding of tools like spreadsheets to help provide the calculations.

Some consumers find financial planning daunting because it's complex and can trigger anxiety about the future. A number of firms offer excellent online financial planning calculators for free, but it can be challenging to deal with all the assumptions those free tools make. (See patrickgeddes.co/transparent-investing for some recommendations.)

An advisor might say:

Many investors simply won't go through the financial planning process themselves, in spite of plenty of readily available information, both online and in books. People talk about sitting down and doing it themselves, but they often balk at the challenge. Our expertise makes this process easier, giving you the information you need to plan for your future.

For many investors, paying for financial planning is a wise investment since they're buying access to expertise they really need. However, as a savvy consumer, you should avoid letting your need for financial planning lead you to pay high fees for ongoing money management that you don't need. Some wealth managers prefer to bundle planning with investing for this very reason: the advisors don't *want* consumers to be able to separate the useful services (like planning) from the ones less likely to add value (like active portfolio management) given that the latter earns them so much more.

Many tasks and burdens of investing can be simplified and even eliminated by implementing the simple approach advocated by the transparent investing philosophy. For example, you don't need to pay for a wealth manager to research potential asset managers if you just go with indexing. Investment advisors often paint a picture of investing as much more difficult than it really needs to be.

Financial planning doesn't have to be terribly complicated, but it's often challenging enough that paying for advice can be the right choice. Those willing to study up on financial planning basics or use online calculators can do this part themselves; for those who find such calculators intimidating or don't feel they have the time or confidence to master the essentials, paying a professional might be a smart move.

2. One-Off Financial Decisions

Closely related to financial planning are *one-off* financial decisions: specific situations that aren't as simple as setting up an optimal portfolio. While much of the advice for investors in books or online focuses on creating ideal portfolios, these recommendations don't prove as helpful at resolving questions like:

- How should a pension affect my asset allocation?
- Should I use excess cash to pay down my mortgage or should I invest it?
- Is it worthwhile to pay the taxes caused by converting my active portfolio to indexing?
- What's the best kind of retirement savings plan if I'm self-employed?

An advisor might say:

Investors often find it hard to frame their one-off decisions in the context of their overall financial plan or current portfolio. We can help address these issues since we know their financial situation and have the expertise to provide good advice.

It's true that it can be challenging to put such decisions in the right financial framework and choose the path that best fits an investor's situation. And while these decisions do involve the future, the choices don't require a crystal ball, allowing a professional advisor to skip the wizard act. The challenge lies in finding an advisor to help with one-off situations without paying for what may be unnecessary ongoing money management.

3. Trading and Reporting (Hassle Reduction)

Some consumers are just not into the do-it-yourself route and are willing to pay when it makes their lives easier. This is a perfectly valid choice as long as you understand two things before making it.

First, you should know precisely how much you're paying for the privilege and be comfortable with spending that amount just to avoid a little hassle. Second, you should understand how simple and low-hassle a portfolio can be with a basic collection of just a few index funds. (Remember, it's a myth that a great portfolio needs to be complicated.)

An advisor might say:

Investors often want to outsource the burden of administering their portfolios. We can take this weight off your shoulders, saving you the time and hassle.

Making a choice to delegate unwanted tasks to a professional can represent a sound consumer decision. Keep in mind, though, that a wealth advisor may have an incentive to persuade you that you're settling for less with too simple a portfolio, hence the need to hire them so they can add, and then manage, more complexity. Simple portfolios of three or four index funds can deliver a great investment solution without much administrative burden.

How do you know whether you should pay to outsource the administrative service? As an analogy, I don't change the oil in my car; I pay someone else to do it. However, I understand what's involved in the process, and I comprehend that I'm paying $30 for someone to take care of that mess for me. If it were to cost me $20,000 each time I have my oil changed, I would certainly figure out how to climb under my car with a drip pan to do that grimy job myself. Incidentally, changing your oil every three months is a lot messier and more time-consuming than monitoring a simple portfolio of index funds, which might require a couple of hours every one or two years (and without getting your clothes greasy).

4. Hand-Holding (Behavioral Finance)

Investing can appear pretty scary, with a lot at stake and little under your control. As we've already learned, your brain and body's natural responses to stress and anxiety predispose you to making decisions that feel safer in the short term, but may not be wise for the long term.

Hand-holding by advisors can help consumers avoid costly mistakes, like buying at market peaks and then selling everything after the disastrous blow-ups that inevitably come. Furthermore, advisors can nudge you in the right direction when a big financial decision feels overwhelming to the point of inertia.

An advisor might say:

Consumers panic in rough market conditions and we can talk them through the rough spots or, conversely, talk them down from overly enthusiastic moves during market highs. In addition, lots of consumers aren't into the do-it-yourself regime, and they need help getting past things like procrastination and decision-making paralysis. We help consumers with these challenges.

It's accurate to say that we can be our own worst enemies psychologically, so anything advisors do that assuages these self-harming financial behaviors benefits consumers. I've heard from a number of ethical advisors that this hand-holding represents the biggest value advisors provide, a claim I find plausible. However, only some investors really need this worthwhile support; others have the resiliency to ride through rough markets without making foolish decisions and therefore don't need any hand-holding.

This self-assessment can prove tricky, though, as some investors overestimate their tolerance for stomach-lurching market drops. One way to self-assess this is to look at your investing history. If you've ridden through bad markets like 2008 to 2009 without selling, you've likely got the discipline to ride out the storms on your own.

5. Initial Asset Allocation

Just setting up a well-balanced portfolio of a mix of asset classes can solve a lot of the confusion consumers face when looking at their existing portfolios or at constructing a new one from scratch. (Note here that we're just talking about getting the asset allocation set up, not monitoring or managing it on an ongoing basis.)

An advisor might say:

Consumers don't really know how to build a well-diversified portfolio, and we can help provide that valuable service. Many investors also don't understand risk well, and we can guide them to the right balance of risk and return to fit their specific situation.

In terms of setting up a portfolio, providing a target asset allocation can be very helpful to a wide range of consumers.

Let's take three different types of investors who are trying to build a portfolio on their own. The first one, Investor A, reads my advice in the next chapter on setting up a good asset allocation for a time horizon of thirty years and settles on 80 percent risky assets (like stocks) and 20 percent safer assets (like bonds) after determining she can endure a fair amount of stock market upheaval. Assuming Investor A really will stick with that allocation through bad stock markets, that's probably a good allocation for her, with no need to hire a wealth advisor if picking the initial asset allocation is the only motivation for consulting an expert.

Our second investor, Investor B, however, goes a bit crazy with assessing her own risk tolerance and assumes that in practice she needs to avoid almost all risk over the same thirty-year time horizon. Investor B picks an asset allocation of 30 percent risky and 70 percent safer. While it benefits her long-term financial health to make sure she doesn't get into investments so risky that she won't be able to endure the roller coaster ride, for almost all investors with a thirty-year time horizon, that asset allocation is much too tame. Investor B may not be able to tolerate as high a risk profile as Investor A, but 30 percent risk and 70 percent safer is a dumb choice given her time horizon. A good advisor would help her find a comfortable middle ground that doesn't sacrifice as much potential for growth.

Our third investor, Investor C, also goes too far with risk tolerance, but in her case, she chooses too much risk. Let's say she has a two-year time horizon but thinks that 100 percent risky sounds like a great allocation because it offers the highest expected return on average. While this is an accurate assessment of risky assets, it's a ghastly choice for a two-year time horizon. Again, any decent wealth manager would try to get Investor C to see how ridiculous her risk choice is for a time horizon so short that she won't recover in the case of a bad market. Instead, they would suggest something much safer.

What choice should you make for your own portfolio? If you go through the steps on asset allocation in the next chapter and end up with something within the appropriate ranges defined there, you may not need a wealth manager to help you with your asset allocation. If you end up outside the recommended ranges, then you might, like Investors B or C, need some help to nudge you to reasonable allocations. (Note that I'm just talking about asset allocation here. The actual selection of asset managers, a.k.a., security selection, is, as the doorkeeper at the Land of Oz would put it, a horse of a different color.)

6. Education on More Obscure Investment Concepts or Techniques

In addition to being scary, investing can be confusing. In this sense, advisors do play a useful educational role in terms of helping a consumer more clearly understand investing from the terms to the different markets to special savings programs such as 529 plans.

An advisor might say:

Consumers find investment terms and details confusing, and part of our job is providing explanations that raise their level of understanding. For example, most investors may not understand the math behind risk diversification or more uncommon investment approaches like "back door" Roth IRA contributions.

For some of these concepts, you can't just look them up on Google and find the best solution to your particular investment challenge. This is where we add value in an advising role.

Sometimes it's a relief to have an expert (who knows your specific situation) to consult when you have to deal with a confusing concept or term. Educating consumers empowers them, and empowered consumers are a wondrous sight to behold.

Nonetheless, as a consumer you still need to be careful about whether you're getting the right *kind* of education. You need to hear about things like fees, but you may not need to know about fancy and expensive strategies that benefit the advisor but not you. In other words, you need to be educated about the personal health benefits of broccoli and how attempts to sell you on that tasty chocolate cake can harm your financial health.

For example, let's say you want to learn more about options, which are somewhat complicated securities that give you the right to buy or sell another security at a certain price. The Broccoli answer might start with something along the lines of, "First, I'll explain how they work technically, and we can look at some situations where options can help you manage risk. Then I'll point out how they can cost a lot more to trade than stocks—you need to understand the explicit and implicit costs before using options." This response makes for good education about a complicated subject.

The Chocolate Cake answer, on the other hand, will sound more like this: "I'm glad you asked about options, as my firm offers some excellent and successful option strategies that can protect you on the downside and also generate more income for you."

Any time an advisor talks only about the benefits of a strategy and not the trade-offs, a little alarm bell should go off in your mind. The advisor may be thinking to themselves, "I don't have any obligation to explain that I make much more money for myself by pushing options strategies than I do pushing boring old indexing."

7. Taxes

For investors who hold taxable accounts (generally anything not inside a retirement account like a 401(k), 403(b), or IRA), the impact of taxes on investing is enormously important, though it can prove complicated. The cost of ignoring the tax impact can be much higher than even fees. However, as we've seen with a lot of issues, wealth managers can do either great good or great harm when it comes to taxes, meaning they provide both useful and suspect services in this area.

An advisor might say:

Investors frequently make poor decisions that lower their after-tax wealth because they may not fully understand all the tax implications. We add a lot of value by helping them make optimal choices.

And as with education about more obscure investment concepts, the tax implications of investing provide opportunities for enormous value added by advisors, but also great cost when advisors dismiss the tax impact, as they frequently do.

Aperio Group was founded as one of the few investment firms to focus heavily on after-tax results, and I know well just how much extra wealth can come from quality tax analysis and expertise. I also know just how costly sexy strategies like active management and hedge funds are from a tax perspective.

Listed below are some of the many ways advisors can improve your after-tax wealth with careful management of the tax impact:

- Placing certain investments within IRAs or other tax-deferred vehicles, ideally building an optimal portfolio when measured after tax.

- Taking advantage of 529 plans and other tax-deferred structures for education expenses.

- Emphasizing the tax benefits of indexing over most active strategies.

- For very wealthy investors, understanding estate tax and optimizing the best way to bequeath the greatest wealth after both income and estate tax.

- Taking full advantage of various trust structures, where applicable.

- Choosing optimal philanthropic strategies in terms of maximizing tax deductions, which lowers your tax liability.

- Planning your social security payments to make sure you avoid tipping yourself into a higher tax bracket inadvertently.

You don't need to understand all these concepts, but they represent valid opportunities for a wealth advisor to improve your portfolio, especially if you pay the highest tax rate because of your income, in which case taxes matter a lot.

If these benefits represent some good tax recommendations, how might an advisor harm your portfolio from the tax side? The damage comes as a result of advisors ignoring the tax impact of various strategies. I once heard an otherwise excellent wealth manager confess that they didn't *want* their clients to understand the tax implications of the hedge fund strategies the advisor was using. Why not? Because the returns after tax were far less appealing than the pre-tax performance the clients were seeing, and the manager didn't want to tarnish the appeal by telling the truth.

The investment industry exhibits a strong allergic reaction to incorporating the tax impact, and I would argue this is because the sexiest (and most expensive) strategies, like active stock picking, look so much worse when they're analyzed after tax. Keep in mind that your advisor doesn't have to pay the extra taxes on those investments; you do.

The challenge for you as a consumer lies in how the same advisor who provides lots of value through tax expertise, like in the list above, may then put you in tax-inefficient strategies that look awful when measured accurately to include the tax impact. How can you tell the difference? Remain open to the kinds of suggestions listed above, but ask whether your advisor measures returns *after* tax (to which the answer is likely to be no). Ask them how their various recommendations look when measured after tax, especially the more active or complicated ones. If they hem and haw and try to steer you away from that line of questioning or claim it's too complicated, that's a bad sign.

Suspect Services

Now let's turn to the suspect services offered by advisors—mainly, the facts and data that certain advisors might not want their clients to understand clearly.

1. Initial Selection of Active Asset Managers

Wealth managers who promote active management do so on the promise that they can pick asset managers who will perform better than the market. Of course, this concept appeals to us all, because who would settle for average when the alternative is superior performance? As we learned in chapter 6, though, on average, the asset management industry has proven it lacks the ability to predict the future by picking the securities that will beat the market.

An advisor might say:

We're experienced professionals who know the financial markets and how to select excellent asset managers. While there's no guarantee that these managers will continue to beat their benchmarks in the future, our firm's research process carefully screens only the best managers with proven track records.

There's no doubt as to the emotional appeal of this argument—the problem is that the research data don't support it. Furthermore, remember that wealth managers are picking asset managers who've beaten the market in the past, not those who will necessarily do so in the future.[45] There's a reason why most large firms, including institutional pension consultants, won't publish a track record of their recommended asset managers' performance *after those managers are hired*. Instead, you only see the track record that led to the manager being selected.

When I hear wealth managers claim that the industry's failure doesn't affect their own prowess at predicting, I'm reminded of the fictional town of Lake Wobegon from the radio show *A Prairie Home Companion*, where "all the children are above average." Everyone being above average may appeal to us emotionally, but unfortunately, the math doesn't work that way.

2. Ongoing Portfolio Management

Beyond the initial selection of a portfolio, consumers like the idea of a professional watching over their account on an ongoing basis. It just seems too risky *not* to have someone monitoring it regularly.

An advisor might say:

Consumers ask us to provide reassurance by monitoring accounts, which we take seriously. Financial markets change constantly, and we provide useful expertise in navigating treacherous waters.

Ongoing portfolio management presents a tricky issue, since there are both valid and invalid reasons to pay for this service.

For example, investment managers do offer the benefit of what is known as *rebalancing*, which means bringing a portfolio back into line with its targeted asset allocation. Basically, this means that when stocks rise significantly, an investor's stock percentage increases beyond the target, meaning they need to sell stocks and buy another asset class, like bonds.

Regular rebalancing has been shown to provide value over the long run. However, an investor may or may not need an outside advisor to take care of that task. Furthermore, disciplined rebalancing is different from an advisor claiming to improve a portfolio by actively tweaking the asset allocation based on market conditions.

3. Market Timing

Advisors like to use the natural volatility of equity markets as a way to intimidate consumers into wanting their assets managed. Popular investment magazines sell a lot of copy with headlines like "The 8 Funds You Need in These Turbulent Times," as if financial markets aren't always at risk of becoming turbulent. It's a reassuring message, that an expert will guide your portfolio through up-and-down markets, being more aggressive when markets rise and less so when they decline.

An advisor might say:

Consumers worry about the risk inherent in equity markets, and we reassure them. Would you want your entire net worth floating around unmanaged during stormy market conditions? Most investors lack the time and skill to maintain close attention to their portfolios through market fluctuations, so they trust us to do it for them.

As we've already discussed, having your hand held during stormy weather may provide real benefit, especially if it keeps you from doing something foolish like selling out during a down market. However, presuming that your wealth manager can predict market moves better than you can provides a false sense of security.

Again, it's important to keep in mind that there's a lot out there that will make you feel nervous about doing anything other than hiring someone to watch over your portfolio. The key word here is "feel." Don't let your emotions cloud the truth of the data, or you may pay for a feeling without getting anything substantive, like higher returns or lower risk.

4. Selling You Insurance

Sometimes advisors can bundle together different services, like insurance of all kinds, that provide extra convenience for you. However, consumers need to be sure they're getting the best insurance for their needs versus the best insurance for their advisor's income.

An advisor might say:

Insurance can be complicated, and we have the expertise to combine insurance needs with investments. This can provide valuable protection across a wide range of situations.

Some types of insurance, like property, health, term life, or disability, don't often overlap with portfolio management, and therefore present less conflict of interest when sold by the same people who manage your portfolio. You still need to check if you're paying too high a premium for such insurance, but in general, you can categorize these types in the "Useful Services" section above.

With cash-value life insurance and variable annuities, however, consumers face a serious problem, as products that include a cash value at the end of a policy's term are often more about generating high fees than solving a valid insurance need for the consumer. Consumers who need life insurance should default first to low-cost term insurance and then choose life insurance with cash value only if it proves to be superior. Term life insurance is analogous to indexing in that every consumer should default to the cheaper and simpler solution first and move to a more expensive and complex choice only after making sure that it's worth the extra outlay.

In fairness, specific situations do exist in which cash-value life insurance can be worthwhile when measured on the basis of after-tax cash flows, especially for the very wealthy. Nonetheless, in my experience, such situations arise far less often than those selling insurance products tend to acknowledge.

Not surprisingly, the financial services industry prefers the products that earn them more in commissions, so cash-value life insurance gets pushed on you in a lot of situations in which you're worse off from, you guessed it, higher fees. Variable annuities even more rarely justify their typically high (and sometimes hidden) costs.[46]

Advice Beyond Basic Asset Classes

For those with net liquid assets of more than, say, $5 million, advisors often argue that while indexing may work for investments in the public equity markets, advisors can provide value in alternative asset classes such as hedge funds, private equity, or real assets such as natural resources or real estate.

These alternative asset classes can provide great benefit in terms of risk, return, and diversification. However, they're not any more immune than regular stocks and bonds to the danger of getting pitched as rare and sexy strategies, in this case available only to a privileged few. In fact, because some of those strategies are so complicated and charge such extremely high fees, investors need to remain particularly vigilant in the face of seductive sales pitches.

I urge anyone investing in these to bear in mind the same warning about the importance of fees that apply to publicly traded securities. Furthermore, I recommend following the advice offered by David Swensen when he was the Chief Investment Officer of Yale University. The *Institutional Investor* website quoted Swensen as counseling any investor with less than $200 million to stick with passive. He said, "Picking successful active managers is difficult for endowments of all sizes, especially in venture capital and absolute returns."[47] Amen to that.

Aren't Index Funds Boring?

When describing their services, advisors might try to add one last point in their favor by claiming that index funds are boring compared to active management. My response to that claim is to surrender completely. No matter how much you might try to dress them up, index funds are still dull as dishwater.

I fully acknowledge that I'm urging you to pick something boring when you could have chocolate cake instead: you won't impress anyone at a party by bragging about your portfolio of all index funds. You'll just have to console yourself with the fact that, on average, you'll have as much as twice the wealth in thirty years compared to your friends who continue to chase returns and pay the high fees for active management.

What Services Should I Buy?

Looking at the lists of useful and suspect services offered by wealth managers, it can be hard to figure out whether it's wise to try this investing stuff on your own or it's better to hire professional help. As you determine which services you really need, your decision will be driven by how much confidence, interest, and time you have available, as well as your ability to stay disciplined during market downturns.

Based on the active (or Chocolate Cake) approach, you might presume that you need a lot of time and interest in investing to handle your own portfolio. However, the Transparent Investing approach reduces the burden on you so that you might reconsider the required commitment, as shown in the following table.

Table 9. Transparent Investing Approach

Factor	Transparent Investing Approach
Confidence	You should be more confident in the solution.*
Interest	If you're bored now, you'll still be bored after educating yourself.
Time	Drastically reduces time requirement.
Emotions	Increased awareness of volatility helps reduce panic.

*You should not be more confident in your predictive ability.

Your tolerance for doing it yourself may actually be higher than you'd suspect at first blush. After learning how simple the solution can be and how important fees are, you might find you're more open to it. Alternatively, you may still dislike or fear the prospect of doing it yourself, but then at least you'll be clear as to why you're paying a professional.

Unfortunately, you face the additional challenge of not only figuring out which services you need and which to avoid but also ascertaining how to get *only* what you need, given that the way the industry gets paid can make it harder for you. To make a restaurant analogy, while you should approach the challenge like ordering à la carte from the menu, the industry may only offer you complete meals, so you don't have the option of skipping the courses you don't want.

How Do You Know If You Need to Hire an Advisor?

Now that we've identified the components that go into the decision of whether to hire a wealth manager, here's a framework to help you make that choice.

Exercise 1. DIY vs. Advisor Scorecard

As a first step, enter a score for yourself on a scale of 1 to 5 for each service listed below, with a 1 meaning "I don't really see much benefit from that service" and a 5 meaning "I shouldn't go without that service."

Service	Score 1 to 5
Financial Planning	
One-Off Financial Decisions	
Hassle Reduction (trading and reporting)	
Initial Asset Allocation	
Education	
Tax Advice around Investing	
Total Score from Services	

Now, move to the four items below and score them again on a 1 to 5 scale, but in the *reverse order* this time, where a 1 means "I have a high inclination (natural tendency) toward this or the ability to provide it on my own," and a 5 means "I don't have any inclination toward this or the ability to provide it on my own."

Personal Inclination	Score 1 to 5
Confidence*	
Interest or Discipline to Act*	
Time*	
Emotions (score low if you've got a strong stomach, high if you're prone to sell in a down market)	
Total Score from Personal Inclination	

*Note that for confidence, interest/discipline, or time, you should determine your appetite or availability not for the complicated portfolio you might have previously presumed you needed but rather for a simple mix of a few investments based mainly on indexing for stocks, for which you don't need to do much beyond letting it sit there untouched over decades.

Combine the two scores:

Sum of Services Score and Inclination Score	

And compare your total score to the table below:

Score	Suggested Approach
40–50	You have little appetite for DIY and should seek an advisor.
30–40	You're inclined to hire an advisor, but you should consider whether you might try it on your own. At the very least, study the recipe guide for DIY in the next chapter so you'll be a better consumer.

20–30	There may be some issues where hired help would be useful, but you'd likely be fine managing your own portfolio. Interview wealth advisors to see if you find a good fit, and if not, try it on your own. An hourly arrangement might also work well for you.
10–20	You're inclined to manage your own portfolio. Seeking advice on a retainer or hourly basis might still be worthwhile, but it's unlikely you need a professional to manage your assets.

Obviously, this questionnaire provides oversimplified guidance as to whether you should try managing a portfolio for yourself, since this decision has a lot of moving parts and a book has its limitations in providing personalized advice. To account for this, feel free to overweight or underweight the scoring to reflect your own situation. Rather than seeking a single "correct choice," think of your results as a framework to help you decide based on what you need and what the investment industry actually provides.

A Final Note on What Active Management Costs You

As you try to wrestle with which services you actually want as a consumer and whether you feel up to building a portfolio yourself, let's clarify one last point on the total costs of active management.

First, we already know from the research on indexing that active, on average, destroys value. Based on the research data, we'll assume that active trails passive by about 1.0 percent per year in lost returns.

This by itself provides a pretty powerful argument, but for the second layer of costs, let's assume you're hiring a wealth advisor solely because you think that person can pick the strategies that will beat the market, not for the more valid reasons we've just covered. According to AdvisoryHQ, the average fee for a wealth manager for a $1 million portfolio is about 1.0 percent.[48] So now the statistics show you're earning 1.0 percent less for active, plus another 1.0 percent on top of that to pay a wealth advisor to pick winning strategies.

But we can't stop here, as there's a third layer of costs involved in active management: taxes. If you pay taxes on your investment earnings (which you do on all taxable accounts), the average drag for high-income investors can be as high as 1.6 percent per year,[49] based on research from Aperio Group. We'll round that number down to 1.0 percent since not everyone may face high state taxes, though even then, it still reflects the highest tax bracket.

How much do all these avoidable fees harm the growth of your portfolio? Picture two equally competent runners competing in a long-distance race—let's say it's a marathon, just to emphasize how much your wealth can suffer over long time periods. Now, ask one of them to carry a small backpack that represents the *cost drag* to returns under active management (that's a 1.0 percent penalty weight). Next, add a second backpack with another 1.0 percent drag due to paying a wealth manager (again, assuming you're hiring not for the valid services but only for earning higher returns). Finally, for your taxable accounts, if you're in the top tax bracket, add a third backpack on the same runner to represent the 1.0 percent tax drag from capital gains caused by active management.

How badly do those three extra backpacks slow down the one runner, compared to the one without them? Let's convert the percentages to actual dollars over a thirty-year time horizon. To emphasize the difference, we'll assume we're comparing two aggressive investors with 100 percent asset allocation in stocks that earn 7 percent per year over that period before the extra cost burdens.

Now, the Broccoli runner—with indexing and no wealth manager—will earn the full 7 percent while the burdened Chocolate Cake runner will earn only 4 percent a year after subtracting out 1 percent per year for each of our three backpacks.

How much better off will the unburdened runner perform? This table shows the results.

Table 10. Illustrated Cost Drag

	Active/Chocolate Cake Runner	Passive/Broccoli Runner
Expected return from 100% stocks	7.0%	7.0%
Extra cost drag from three backpacks	-3.0%	0.0%
Net return after cost burdens	4.0%	7.0%
Starting balance	$100,000	$100,000
Ending balance after thirty years*	$324,340	$761,226

*Ending value ignores any tax on final liquidation, which applies for assets you might pass through an estate. The actual tax penalty would be less if you include the tax impact of final liquidation.

While I've acknowledged that the passive approach can seem boring, ending up with twice as much money should still provide some real satisfaction. Wealth managers who say they can overcome the 3 percent in average cost drag by timing the market or recommending the best asset managers should be met with real skepticism, given the absurdly long odds that they can outperform by that much.

In fact, let's take a closer look at those odds. In a study analyzing the historical performance of more than 4,500 US mutual funds between 2005 and 2015, the odds of beating comparable Vanguard index and other low-fee mutual funds after paying taxes was 5 percent—meaning an investor faced a *95 percent chance* of trailing. (The study assumed a high-income taxable investor who sells at the end of the holding period.)[50]

Table 11. Odds of Winning with Active Investing

	Odds of Winning with Active	Average Performance per Annum vs. Indexing
Active Winners	5%	+0.76%
Active Losers	95%	-1.17%
All Active		-0.96%

Source: "Is Active Alpha Enough to Cover Taxes?" based on research originally from Morningstar.[51]

Figure A. 95% vs. 5% Performance

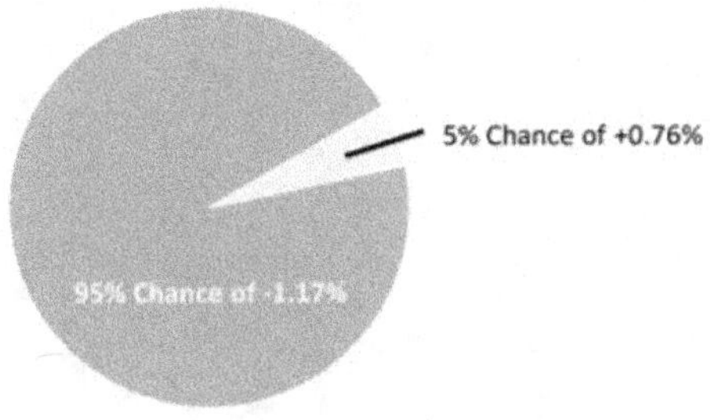

The combination of all the ways active management can leave you with less money makes it clear that all investors should at least default first to indexing, and only venture into active with the full realization that the probability of beating the market remains extremely low. Thinking you're smarter than the market bodes poorly for your portfolio.

Chapter 9

How to Do It Yourself

IF YOU TOOK THE SELF-ASSESSMENT quiz and determined you might want to build a portfolio on your own, this chapter will provide the steps to do that. And if you're on the fence or leaning toward hiring someone, the following information will still help you understand the process better.

Here's a table showing the seven steps to building a DIY portfolio, along with their level of complexity. We'll go through each in detail in this chapter.

Table 12. 7 Steps to a DIY Portfolio

Step	Action	Topics Covered	Complexity
1	Financial Planning	What are you saving for? What's your time horizon?	Moderate

2	Determining Your Risk Tolerance	What's your risk tolerance?	Basic
3	Asset Allocation	How much should you invest in risky assets like stocks versus safer assets like bonds? What's the inflation risk?	Basic
4	Choosing Index Funds	What funds should you buy? Which benchmark should you use?	Basic
5	Dealing with Taxes	What's your current allocation across taxable versus non-taxable accounts? How can you build the most tax-efficient portfolio?	Moderate
6	Deciding Whether to Include Impact Investing	What if you want your portfolio to reflect your values on environmental or social issues?	Moderate
7	Ongoing Portfolio Management	How should you manage your portfolio through different market conditions?	Basic

Do-It-Yourself Step #1: Financial Planning

Irrespective of your level of wealth, the financial planning process includes deciding how much you need to save per year to meet those goals or, coming at it from another angle, how much you can spend per year—especially in retirement—given a certain size of portfolio.

Defining your goals is a standard first step for investing, but many investors still skip it and jump ahead to the investments themselves. Picking the best investment strategy without knowing your goals is like choosing a car without knowing how you plan to use it.

Many people start with a variety of goals, which is why it can be helpful to separate out different portions of your portfolio for different uses. For example, you might want to save for a down payment on a house you intend to buy in two years. For this goal, risky assets like stocks provide a terrible investment for such a short time horizon, with cash and maybe some short-term bonds being the best choice. Alternatively, a goal like saving for retirement in, say, thirty years generally implies a much riskier allocation, where cash is a bad idea because it's performed so poorly over long time horizons.

For specific short-term goals, like saving for a down payment on a house two years from now, it's fine to have a separate goal with a pool of money just for that purpose. However, I recommend combining long-term goals into one blended time horizon, looking at your total portfolio as a single pool of investments rather than separate ones for different goals.

Retirement planning, as I mentioned, stands out as one of the most important motivations for this step of the process. Wealth managers often use the rule of thumb that you should be able to withdraw 4 percent per year from your portfolio safely and never run out of money. There's been some discussion lately, however, that because bond yields are so low, this payout standard may actually be too high; there's also research showing it's too low, because with a 4 percent withdrawal rate, investors often end up with too big a cushion (meaning they lived *too* stingy a lifestyle). While it's not perfect, if you're looking at planning for your retirement from a very high level, the 4 percent withdrawal rate still proves useful.

How should you approach doing your own financial planning, whatever your goals or level of wealth? If you're skilled with spreadsheets, you can try building your own forecasts, but there are also many financial planning tools available online, many of them free. The best ones provide the probability of achieving a specific goal rather than a single forecasted result. These forecasts across a range of outcomes use what's called Monte Carlo simulation, which looks not at a single version of the future but at thousands of different versions and then analyzes how often the plan hits its goal.

For example, if you have a 65 percent chance of reaching your retirement goal, you'll run out of money in more than a third of outcomes, which, for most of us, is a worrisome bet on the future. On the other hand, almost no one will have a portfolio big enough to guarantee that in 100 percent of the possible outcomes of the future you'll still have enough. Just as a rule of thumb, reaching your goals 90 percent of the time should provide a good level of comfort, but for most people, 70 percent leaves too much opportunity for unpleasant financial surprises in your future.

Besides forecasting, various websites offer other excellent tools such as cash flow planners, which allow you to input different portfolio amounts and savings rates to help determine how much to save or how much you can spend in retirement. For a current list of my favorite online tools, visit patrickgeddes.co/transparent-investing.

If you try using online tools and find the process daunting, financial planning may be an area where you want to seek help. Of all the challenges of doing it yourself, the planning part is one of the most complicated. This may seem counterintuitive (it seems like it should be much easier than building a portfolio on your own), but remember, out of self-interest, the investment industry *wants* you to think that building a portfolio is complicated.

Do-It-Yourself Step #2: Determining Your Risk Tolerance

A standard step in assembling the right portfolio for you, whether you're working with a wealth manager or doing it yourself, requires assessing your risk tolerance. While it's an unfortunately hypothetical process, the basic goal of determining how much risk you can bear tries to capture exactly what you'll do in a bad stock market, i.e., will you sell out when you're watching your account balance plummet?

Gauging your own risk tolerance is a helpful exercise, but its real value depends less on guessing in advance what you'll do during the next bad market drop and more on changing your expectations regarding whether or not you can avoid such a drop. While you should generally run screaming in horror from an investment manager who promises a sure thing, it's pretty close to a sure thing that if you're a long-term investor in stocks, at some point you'll have to endure a horrible, gut-wrenching downturn. The more you internalize that watching your portfolio crater at some point is the price of admission, the less freaked out you'll be when it actually happens.

Many websites offer questionnaires to help you determine how much market volatility you can actually stomach. While these prove helpful in framing how to *think* about what you'd do, they can't accurately predict exactly how you'll behave, which means you're stuck with your own self-awareness.

While it isn't easy to know how you'll react in the moment, I recommend trying to imagine bad and worst-case scenarios. While this might sound unpleasant, it can help you digest the fact that disturbing stock market drops come with investing in stocks. Bad periods like 2000 to 2002 and 2008 to 2009 happen, regardless of all the shocked reactions of "How could this be possible?" This kind of shock and panic can hurt your wealth, since it makes you sell out of stocks when they're plummeting.

If you have no idea how you might behave as an investor during a bad bear market, it could be a good idea to hire a wealth manager. The strength of your stomach lining will also affect how high a percentage of your portfolio you should allocate to risky assets, as we'll see in step 3. But first, we need to briefly discuss the common danger of not taking *enough* market risk to account for inflation.

Market Risk versus Inflation Risk

Time lowers the chances of losing money in risky assets. In general, the longer your time horizon, the lower your likelihood of a negative return over a given period. The table below shows the historical range of rolling period real returns—that is, pre-tax returns adjusted for inflation—from 1926 to 2020.

Table 13. Historical Range of Rolling Period Real Returns

	Total Annualized Real Returns Over Different Holding Periods, 1926–2020	
Asset Allocation	**Returns After 1 Year**	**Returns After 20 Years**
100% Money Market (low market risk)	High +13.41% Average +0.48% Low -16.14%	High +2.95% Average +0.23% Low -3.19%

100% Stocks (high market risk)	High	+181.51%	High	+13.85%
	Average	+9.13%	Average	+7.03%
	Low	-63.99%	Low	+0.27%

Note: Due to compounding, the average one-year returns may differ significantly from the annualized twenty-year average returns. Cash reflects one-month US T-Bills, stocks the S&P 500, inflation the US CPI. Source: data from Dimensional Fund Advisors, calculations by me. Figures shown reflect returns through June 30, 2020.

Here, we see the high, average, and low returns based on one-year versus twenty-year periods between the years 1926 and 2020. As you can see, cash is a great investment for a one-year time horizon compared to stocks because the risk of loss is so much lower. However, for a twenty-year time horizon, stock performance is much better than cash.

There are two main takeaways from this table. First, over the average twenty-year period, cash earned basically no real return, due to inflation. Therefore, while cash sounds like a safe investment, it's awful in hedging against inflation risk over the long term.

Second, the twenty-year return *low* for stocks across nearly a century was still higher than the *average* return for cash. This is why stocks make such sense for the long haul, assuming you can endure the bumpy ride.

Most investors think of risk in terms of short-term volatility—basically, whether they'll lose money in the short term. However, over periods of more than ten years or so, inflation becomes the true risk, even if it was relatively tame during the thirty-five years from 1985 to 2020. If you focus too much on keeping your portfolio from losing money simply in terms of the nominal value, you may end up losing money when measured in terms of purchasing power. This table highlights the common danger of not taking enough market risk in order to offset inflation.

If you're going to build your portfolio yourself, you'll have to decide on the right balance between risky and safer assets for, say, a long-term portfolio you're planning on holding for at least twenty years. This may feel daunting, but there's a helpful rule of thumb that can make the choice less intimidating. Going back for more than half a century, many institutions and individuals have opted for a 60 percent risky and 40 percent safer allocation. In spite of plenty of research showing how out of date this one-size-fits-all approach is, this simple allocation has performed well over time for many situations.

The 60/40 balance presumes a certain level of risk tolerance on your part, namely that you rely on the safer component (which is likely to return less but with a much less bumpy ride) to make you feel more secure when the risky portion drops in value in upsetting ways. If you really have an iron stomach and can survive a market drop (which means not selling at the bottom), going riskier than 60/40 can prove appropriate.

Do-It-Yourself Step #3: Asset Allocation

At this point in the process, your risk tolerance is no longer an abstract idea: you're actually going to pick an asset allocation based on your ability to stomach risk. With this, keep in mind that the best portfolio reflects you and how you're likely to behave, especially since evolution has made investment discipline so hard for us. (Although the more you brace yourself in advance that bad markets are unavoidable, the more you'll be able to tolerate higher risk.)

Asset allocation simply means what percentage of your total portfolio gets deployed to different types of assets. As we've discussed, the basic goal with allocation is to avoid the extremes of too much market risk (so that you can't endure market gyrations, leading you to sell out in a panic) or too little market risk (subjecting you to inflation over decades).

Before discussing how to construct a well-balanced portfolio, it's helpful to define what we mean by asset classes, which are a broad grouping of different types of securities. The simplest approach here is to divide all assets into two main groups: the safer basket and the risky basket.

The Safer Basket

The lowest-risk asset in the safer basket is cash, which is the same thing for our purposes as a money market fund. While most money market funds (except for those that invest exclusively in US Treasury bills) aren't completely free of risk, they're still the safest of all assets outside of a bank deposit or security guaranteed by the federal government.

The other asset in the safer basket is bonds, which are the equivalent of loaning money to corporations or governments. Bonds do bring some risk, although far less than the stock market. Bonds can fluctuate in price, mainly as a function of changes in long-term interest rates.

While there are different types of bonds and bond mutual funds, the simplest distinction for asset allocation is to understand the difference between taxable and tax-exempt bonds. Taxable bonds include corporate bonds and bonds of the US government, although US Treasury bonds are not subject to state income tax. Tax-exempt bonds are also known as municipal bonds ("munis") and include those issued by state or local governments.

The Risky Basket

Stocks and real estate are the most common investments in the risky basket. We'll focus on stocks here, including both US and foreign stocks. Often stocks get further categorized into large companies (large cap) and small companies (small cap), although it isn't necessary to go even to that level of detail.

The simplest and most reliable stock strategies reflect the broadest ownership of all types of stocks. For example, there is some evidence, though it isn't as prevalent as it once was, that smaller US companies bring higher returns, but also higher risk. Therefore, owning a little more in small companies is fine, but if your *entire* stock allocation is small companies, that's a pretty active asset allocation bet that I wouldn't recommend.

For the US stock market, I recommend defaulting to owning the whole thing through a market capitalization index. Similarly, you should own some foreign stocks, at least 20 percent of your stock allocation.

Comparing the Returns for Both Baskets

What have returns been historically for different asset classes? This table shows the historical risk and rates of return for cash, bonds, and stocks, adjusted for inflation (the same thing as "real returns"). Here, the risk (shown as standard deviation) reflects the volatility of real returns averaged over nearly a century.

Table 14. Risk and Return, 1926–2020

	Real Return	Risk (Std. Dev.)
Cash	0.44%	1.81%
Bonds	2.88%	8.79%
Stocks	7.04%	18.66%

Note: Cash reflects one-month US T-Bills, bonds long-term government bonds, stocks the S&P 500, inflation the US CPI. Source: Data from Dimensional Fund Advisors, calculations by me. The standard deviation has been annualized assuming independent monthly observations. Figures shown reflect returns through June 30, 2020. Averages may differ from Table 13 due to compounding over 94.5 years.

How Much Should You Allocate to Risky and Safer?

Getting your basic asset allocation between the two baskets, risky and safer, is the most important decision for your portfolio. If you get this right, the details of how you pick securities matters less. For example, let's say you're twenty-five years old and saving for retirement. If you pick an asset allocation of 20 percent risky and 80 percent safer, that's a terrible long-term plan since your time horizon allows you to earn a much higher return and bear more risk in your circumstances.

This graph shows how much inflation risk increases as the time horizon gets longer.

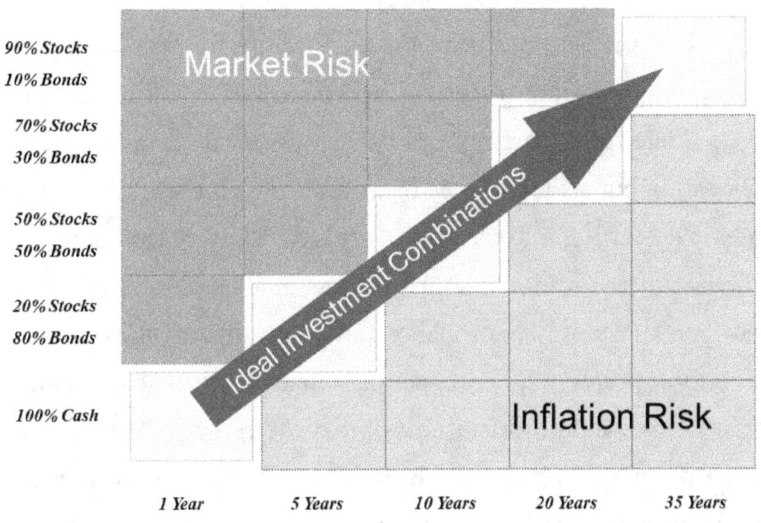

Figure B. Ideal Investment Combinations over Time

This graph oversimplifies the exact portfolio weights, which are flexible, but it illustrates the basic trade-off between the two types of risk and how much more market risk you should bear if you face a longer time horizon.

It's important to note that these asset class recommendations aren't hard and fast. In fact, a wide range of allocations may be appropriate for you, and not all advisors will agree as to the exact one. However, most wealth managers will at least be within the same basic range—you aren't likely to run into a scenario in which some wealth managers recommend 90 percent of your portfolio in riskier assets and others recommend only 20 percent (as long as you're sharing the same information regarding your financial situation and goals).

If you're brand new to asset allocation for your own portfolio, you may want to consider prepackaged investments called target-date funds that not only provide a single diversified asset allocation but also rebalance over time, lowering your risk profile as you get farther into retirement. This rebalancing feature reflects the fact that you should adjust your asset allocation as your time horizon shortens: you probably don't want the same asset allocation for retirement funds at age sixty that you want at age eighty.

Target-date funds are designed for retirement plans, but even if you're planning for broader goals than just retirement, these prefabricated offerings still provide an excellent framework for asset allocation. The only trick here is that for taxable portfolios subject to high tax rates, you may need to start with the same basic proportions but substitute municipal bonds for taxable bonds.

This table shows the asset allocation as of 2021 for a series of Vanguard target-date funds. I include this not to encourage you to invest in target-date funds, necessarily, but to show how asset allocation may vary depending on the time horizon.

Table 15. Vanguard Target-Date Funds Asset Allocation

Time Horizon, in Years	Risky, %	Safer, %
1	0	100
5	20	80
10	50	50
15	60	40
20	70	30
30	83	17
35+	90	10

Except for the one- and five-year horizons, the numbers in this table come from the Vanguard Target Portfolio funds as of 2021. These are funds designed for 401(k) plans to provide one-stop shopping with a diversified blend of risky and safer asset classes. I've assumed that the time horizon for these retirement portfolios falls on average ten years beyond the target date. For a one-year time horizon, the default reflects all cash as the most prudent asset allocation. The five-year number shows the Vanguard LifeStrategy Income Fund, a conservative prepackaged portfolio. Then for time horizons of 10 to 35+ years, the asset allocation reflects the breakdown between stocks (risky) and bonds (safer) in the Vanguard Target Retirement portfolios of various lengths of time horizon.

What might lead you to choose different asset allocations than the simplified table above? Let's start with the reasons you might want to take less risk:

1. It's likely you can't tolerate as much risk as this allocation assumes.

Remember, it's not what you say you'll do that counts, but rather how you actually behave during a big drop in the stock market (by big, let's say a decline of 30 percent or more). This means that while a 90 percent risky allocation over a thirty-five-year time horizon is the right call for many, if you're likely to sell in a bear market, you may not want to have this much in the risky bucket (also called the risky basket).

2. Your wealth compared to your needs is high enough that you can tolerate a lower expected return since it means lower market risk.

If you're lucky enough to be one of the rare people who finds themselves in this situation, in effect you're saying you're willing to take on higher inflation risk to avoid market risk since you may not need a terribly high return to meet your financial goals.

3. You think the market looks overpriced right now, so you intend to maintain a lower risk profile that you'll increase once the market calms down.

As described earlier, this is a form of market timing. I strongly recommend picking a risk allocation you can endure and sticking with it instead. However, if you're looking at the stock market during a period of high valuation and you realize you want a safer portfolio to protect against a big drop, it's fine to go with a safer allocation that you keep in place—just don't fiddle with it based on your assessment of market conditions.

Why might you take more risk than the table above might suggest?

1. You believe you have higher risk tolerance than average, so in order to earn a higher return, you're willing to invest more aggressively.

This may be a perfectly valid reason to take on more risk, but in my experience, investors can significantly overestimate their actual risk tolerance. I've counseled plenty of investors who tell me how high their risk tolerance is—until a market crash, when they panic and significantly lower their risk exposure at exactly the wrong time. Nonetheless, there remain plenty of investors with iron stomachs who can and do tolerate a lot of risk, and over the decades, they get compensated for it.

2. Your portfolio may not be large enough to make it likely that you'll reach your goals without a higher return.

You may need a higher return to achieve your goals, but this comes at the cost of higher risk. Taking more risk than what you can endure during a stock market downturn could lead you to the worst of all outcomes, in which you aim high and then readjust in the middle of a meltdown.

To simplify, rather than presuming a single asset allocation for you based on your time horizon, here are my recommended ranges.

Table 16. Recommended Ranges of Risk

Time Horizon, Years	Risky, %	Safer, %
1	0	100*
5	0–30	70–100
10	20–60	40–80
20+	60–100	0–40

*For a one-year horizon, I'd recommend 100% cash, i.e., no bonds at all. For longer periods, the safer part of a portfolio should comprise bonds.

If you don't think the standard target-date fund allocations are a good fit for you, use the table above to tilt toward safer or riskier. I wouldn't recommend going outside these ranges, however. Remember that you need to balance market risk with inflation risk.

Keep in mind that these recommendations reflect a long-term, usually multi-decade, portfolio. I, like most advisors, also recommend having an emergency fund in cash (not in a retirement account) with three to six months of living expenses that's separate from your long-term portfolio.

Do-It-Yourself Step #4: Choosing Index Funds

After you've determined your target asset allocation, it's time to select the best index funds to represent each asset class.

This brings up another choice: whether to invest in a single pre-packaged solution (like Vanguard's Target Retirement funds) or construct your own collection of separate index funds.

I've chosen Vanguard's Target Retirement funds as the pre-fabricated offerings to share with you for three reasons. First, they combine a mixture of very low-cost index funds into one single fund without any extra layer of fees. Second, the ownership structure effectively makes Vanguard more like a cooperative than a for-profit company. Third, while many fund companies offer prepackaged retirement funds, Vanguard often offers the lowest-cost options.

If you want a simple solution, you can invest all of your assets in this one fund, assuming you have the right time horizon and can tolerate the risk associated with that asset allocation. However, keep in mind that this approach may not be ideal if part of your portfolio is taxable (i.e., not in an IRA or retirement account) and your taxable income is high enough to make municipal bonds a better choice for your safer bucket than taxable bonds.

However, many investors want to go beyond the simplicity of one fund to build their own custom portfolios of index funds. In this case, the Vanguard Target Retirement funds provide an excellent framework to use as you evaluate asset allocation and fees.

Listed below are a few situations in which it's a good idea to go beyond the simplicity of the Target Retirement funds.

Situation #1: High Tax Bracket

Since the Target Retirement funds were designed for tax-exempt accounts like IRAs, all the bond investments are in taxable bonds, which is the best choice if you don't have to pay taxes currently. However, if you have taxable assets and are in a high tax bracket, you should substitute municipal bonds for the taxable bond component.

Situation #2: Mix of Taxable and Tax-Exempt Accounts

To optimally allocate your assets among taxable and tax-exempt accounts, you may need to take advantage of sheltering tax-inefficient assets in retirement accounts. (We'll cover this in the next step.)

Situation #3: More Varied Asset Class Allocation

The Target Retirement funds often do not include allocations to *real assets*, which means real estate and commodities. Many high-net-worth investors have exposure to investment real estate (not including a primary residence). Investors without any additional exposure to real assets can consider a blend of index portfolios that also include real estate investment trusts (REITs) and commodities. Some investors may want to own an even broader range of asset classes beyond real assets, like hedge funds and private equity, often limited to investors with assets in the tens of millions of dollars.

How Much Should You Allocate to Foreign Stocks?

Within the stock portion of your portfolio, one last decision is how much to allocate to US stocks and foreign stocks. While there is some debate over whether the foreign business exposure of US stocks provides full-enough global diversification, I recommend at least some amount of foreign stocks for diversification.

How much foreign stock exposure is enough? Global markets as of 2021 reflect the US as about 58 percent of global stock market value, leaving 42 percent in foreign. Because most US investors will be spending their investments in US dollars, many investors end up overweighting the US stock market compared to the actual worldwide weights.

Almost all investors who own stocks should have at least some foreign stock exposure, but an acceptable exposure can range from 20 percent of your total stock exposure up to as high as the global market weight, about 42 percent as of 2021. The Vanguard Target Retirement funds reflected close to the market capitalization of about 42 percent foreign in 2021.

For my own portfolio, I have about 30 percent, a somewhat arbitrary midpoint. Don't sweat where in that range you should be, although with any foreign investing you should understand that sometimes US markets perform better and sometimes foreign ones do.

Open-End Mutual Fund or Exchange Traded Fund?

Investors can index easily through two different types of fund, a traditional open-end mutual fund (OEF) or an exchange-traded fund (ETF). For an indexed OEF, you usually invest directly through the mutual fund company itself. ETFs, however, trade on stock exchanges just like regular stocks, so you buy and sell them through a brokerage account. For long-term investors, the differences between the two types of index fund are minor, as both offer excellent broadly diversified benchmarks at low fees.

Do-It-Yourself Step #5: Dealing with Taxes

Many investors find income taxes confusing, and people have told me that nothing about investing makes their heads hurt more than thinking about taxes. Unfortunately, the tax code can be fairly complicated, but that's the reality we all face. If this section just makes your eyes glaze over, that's understandable, but hopefully the simple tips provided can still be helpful. Paying attention to taxes can mean you keep a lot more of your money rather than paying it to the government.

In spite of the benefits of focusing on taxes, advisors and money managers too often ignore the effect taxes have on investors, which can be significant. Why do taxes get ignored? For one thing, they complicate investing, but, more importantly, investors are the ones paying the taxes, and advisors and money managers often hope their clients won't understand the drag on returns that come with active management and poor tax planning.

While the historical data of active management versus indexing overwhelmingly favors indexing, the research almost always ignores taxes. And when taxes are included, indexing becomes even more compelling.

The big advantage of indexing is that *you* control the timing of your tax payments from capital gains, not the manager.

With indexing, you, as a taxable investor, can defer taxes and end up with more after-tax wealth, whereas with active management, you're often forced to pay income tax earlier, lowering your after-tax return.

If you already have a portfolio with a lot of unrealized capital gain, it makes sense to pay attention to the capital gain tax effects of selling existing assets in order to rebalance. While I advocate that all investors default to a simple portfolio based on indexing, paying a lot of capital gain tax to do so makes things more complicated. (And of course, complex tax situations arise that require more than the three basic steps explained over the next few pages, but those are beyond the scope of this book.)

As a taxable investor, you have two stages for incorporating the tax impact into your portfolio:

1. Identify the tax status of all your accounts. (This is different from your decision on how much to allocate to risky versus safer.)

2. For taxable accounts, choose between taxable and municipal bonds based on current yields and your tax bracket.

If 100 percent of your assets are held in one type of account, say a 401(k), then you don't have to worry about the tax status, and you can focus on just the asset allocation, ignoring which assets go in which type of account.

Identifying Your Current Allocation by Account Tax Status

The advice in many books and articles on investing presupposes that you're starting out with all cash, looking to create an ideal portfolio. Unfortunately, our financial lives tend to be messy in terms of our current portfolios. Many investors have, for example, a mishmash collection of mutual funds a broker once sold them, a few individual stocks they've picked, more mutual funds in a 401(k) or other retirement account, some IRAs, et cetera.

This is why it's critical at this stage to get a good idea of your total portfolio across all your different accounts, and it's important to think of your portfolio as a whole rather than as individual pieces.

Generally, investment accounts fall into three categories:

1. Taxable accounts

2. Tax-deferred retirement accounts in traditional 401(k), 403(b), 457, or traditional IRA accounts

3. Tax-exempt accounts like Roth 401(k)s or Roth IRAs

For taxable accounts (category #1), you generally have to pay income tax every year on whatever you receive in interest, dividends, capital gains, or other income, and you may have to pay tax on any withdrawals.

For traditional retirement accounts (category #2), funded with income on which you *haven't* yet paid taxes, you still avoid the ongoing tax liability of income earned within the account, but, unlike the Roths, you have to eventually pay taxes upon withdrawal. Remember that all withdrawals from category #2 get taxed eventually at your highest tax rate at the time, whether or not any appreciation resulted from capital gains or ordinary income. For all Roth accounts (category #3), your investment earnings accrue without current tax liability, and then all withdrawals (after a certain holding period) come out tax free as well. That's because they're funded up front with income on which you've already paid taxes.

As you look at your own portfolio, the matrix below can help you categorize all your investments across asset classes (shown in columns) and tax status of accounts (shown in rows). For your current portfolio, fill in the numbers for each type of asset class and account.

For investments that may include more than one asset class, like a balanced mutual fund that might be 60 percent stocks and 40 percent bonds, split each multi-asset-class investment into the specific category before summing up your entire portfolio. For example, if you have $100,000 in your 60/40 balanced fund, enter it as $60,000 in stocks and $40,000 in bonds as if it were two separate pieces.

All different types of stock holdings should be placed in the stocks category, including single stock positions, stock mutual funds, separately managed equity accounts, and the stock portion of any balanced funds.

Additionally, although high-yield bonds (often called "junk bonds") are technically bonds, you should put them in the risky bucket with your stocks. Also, remember that you never want to hold tax-exempt bonds in a tax-advantaged account. The following sections explain this in more detail—including when you should choose taxable or tax-exempt bonds for your bond allocation.

If you need to skip ahead to read through those sections before filling out this worksheet, that's fine, but be sure to come right back and take the time to get these numbers written down now. You'll need them as you progress through the next stages.

Exercise 2. Categorize Investments by Asset Class and Tax Status

		Risky Bucket			Safer Bucket		
Asset Class → *Account Type* ↓		US Stocks	Foreign Stocks	Real Assets & Other	Bonds	Cash	**Total**
Taxable	Taxable Mutual Funds						$_____
	Taxable Brokerage						$_____
	Family Trust						$_____
	Other Taxable						$_____
Tax-Deferred	Tradition-al 401(k) or 403(b)						$_____
	Tradition-al IRA						$_____
	Other Tax-De-ferred						$_____
Tax-Exempt	Roth IRA or Roth 401(k)						$_____
	Total, $						$_____
	Total, %*						100%

*Note: To calculate the percentage of the total, divide the $ amount for each asset class by the total $ amount of the entire portfolio.

Remember the importance of looking at your *entire* portfolio, both by asset allocation and by account type. For example, I once recommended that a friend who had started a new job put 100 percent of her 401(k) investment in taxable bonds (US government and corporate). When she asked me why that wasn't poor diversification, I assured her that her overall portfolio (which I'd helped her design), including all her taxable and tax-exempt accounts, was well diversified *when combined together.*

Once you've looked at your entire portfolio and see changes you need to make, the tempting solution is to simply sell everything you currently own and start over. Unfortunately, taxes can complicate such a realignment because selling holdings in taxable accounts can trigger capital gains, which can be significant if you've held those accounts for a long time.

The basic rule of thumb is that if all your assets are in tax-deferred (qualified) retirement accounts, e.g., 401(k)s or IRAs, and you want to make a change, you can transfer them directly (direct transfer or rollover) without incurring any tax penalty. However, if you have taxable accounts that have appreciated in value and you want to make changes, you need to consider the tax impact of realigning your portfolio.

Again, the breakdown between the safer and risky buckets remains your most important decision, and it's imprudent to maintain too high a risky allocation just to avoid taxes. But let's say you have an active strategy that you now wish were passive. Your decision should be driven by how much capital gains tax you'll incur by selling, as a proportion of the asset's current value. While there are no hard and fast rules, if the gain you'd incur is greater than 50 percent of the asset's current value, it may be better to hold onto a more expensive active strategy rather than take the tax hit to sell it.

Allocating Your Assets in the Most Tax-Efficient Way

After completing do-it-yourself step 3 in this chapter, you should know how much to put in the risky bucket and how much in the safer bucket. Now it's time to determine how to allocate your holdings across your taxable, tax-deferred, and tax-exempt accounts.

Unlike your asset allocation, which you pick based on your time horizon and risk tolerance, the tax status of your accounts is simply a reflection of where you've accumulated any assets, and you will need to work within your current structure. You may change what you put in each type of account, but you almost certainly don't want to make any adjustments like withdrawing early from a tax-advantaged account like an IRA or 401(k).

We'll develop some basic rules for long-term investing as we start allocating different asset classes to the three account types, starting with tax-deferred accounts.

For tax-deferred accounts like a traditional 401(k) or IRA, it's usually best to fill those first with investments that generate a lot of what's called *ordinary income*, which means taxable bonds (especially junk bonds) and REITs. We choose those investments for two reasons. First, they pay out taxable income every year, and it's better to keep them in a tax-deferred account. Second, all withdrawals that come out of tax-deferred accounts get taxed at your highest ordinary income rate. Since you'll eventually pay taxes when you withdraw, you benefit from putting your lower-returning investments, like bonds, in a tax-deferred account to avoid paying the highest rate later.

For tax-exempt Roth accounts, you'll never pay any taxes on withdrawal. Because of that ability to shelter any amount of taxable income on appreciation, it's best to fill Roths first with active stock strategies if you still prefer that route, and second with indexed stocks. We put high-return assets in Roths because that helps us avoid big tax bills when we're in retirement.

Finally, for taxable accounts, fill them first with index stock funds or municipal bonds, depending on your asset allocation and tax bracket, as they're the most tax-efficient strategies.

How do these guidelines work in practice? Let's look at two examples of allocating across taxable and tax-deferred accounts, ignoring tax-exempt Roths for now. In both, let's say you've determined you want 70 percent of your portfolio in the risky bucket and 30 percent in the safer bucket, which we'll simplify to mean 70 percent stocks and 30 percent bonds. You've chosen this allocation based on a combination of your time horizon and risk tolerance. How you implement this 70/30 allocation will depend on the tax status of all your accounts. We'll assume you're using only index funds for the stock allocation.

For example 1, let's say you currently hold 55 percent of your total portfolio in taxable accounts and 45 percent in your 401(k), a tax-deferred account.

Following our rule of filling the tax-deferred account first with taxable bonds, we have capacity of 45 percent, but our asset allocation needs only 30 percent in bonds. Thus we put the entire 30 percent bond allocation in taxable bonds in the tax-deferred account, leaving us with 15 percent leftover capacity that we put in stocks. Then all of the taxable 55 percent goes in stocks, getting us to our 70/30 asset allocation.

This table shows the breakdown.

Table 17. 70/30 Taxable vs. Tax-Deferred Account Allocation, Example 1

	Risky	Safer	Total
Taxable	55%	0%	55%
Tax-deferred	15%	30%	45%
Total Allocation	70%	30%	100%

For example 2, we'll assume the same asset allocation of 70 percent risky/30 percent safer, but this time let's say you currently have only 20 percent of your portfolio in tax-deferred accounts and 80 percent in taxable accounts. Again starting with the tax-deferred account, use up all of the 20 percent in taxable bonds for the same reasons from example 1. Since you need to get to 30 percent safer, though, you'll need to put the remaining 10 percent of your safer investments in your taxable account. (The next section explains whether you should pick taxable or municipal bonds for your taxable account.) That leaves 70 percent remaining capacity in your taxable accounts, which you fill with stock index funds. This table shows the breakdown.

Table 18. 70/30 Taxable vs. Tax-Deferred Account Allocation, Example 2

	Risky	Safer	Total
Taxable	70%	10%	80%
Tax-deferred	0%	20%	20%
Total Allocation	70%	30%	100%

What if we also hold assets in a tax-exempt Roth? Because withdrawals from a Roth account never trigger taxes, we should put the investments with the highest returns there, starting with active stocks (if you still believe in that), then indexed stocks. If you have the choice, minimize holding safer assets in a Roth, as you'll be wasting the advantageous tax treatment better suited for the assets with the highest expected returns. If all your assets are in Roths, then of course it doesn't matter.

Choosing Bonds in Taxable Accounts:
Taxable Bonds versus Tax-Exempt Bonds

Domestic bonds come in two basic flavors: taxable (mainly federal or corporate) and tax-exempt (state or municipal). Here we're talking about the way income from the bond (or bond fund) itself gets taxed, not the account in which it's held. It can be confusing since "taxable" or "tax-exempt" can refer either to a type of account or to a type of bond. (See what I meant about your eyes glazing over?) For tax-deferred or tax-exempt accounts, always choose taxable bonds. For your taxable accounts, the choice between the two types of bonds should be driven mainly by your tax bracket, meaning you'll need to calculate the after-tax yield for each bond type.

To do this, you'll first need to determine your *marginal tax rate*, or the highest tax rate that applies to your ordinary income (not capital gain). This is different from your effective tax rate, which is the overall percentage of your income that goes toward taxes.

As of this book's publication, there are seven federal brackets ranging from tax rates of 10 percent to 37 percent. Each bracket applies to a range of income, depending on how you're filing (e.g., single, married filing jointly). For almost all investors, your income will span several tax brackets: the *highest* bracket that applies to your income is your marginal tax rate. See www.irs.gov for more information.

For example, let's say you're filing your 2021 taxes as a single person and made $60,000 after the standard deduction. This amount spans the first three tax brackets (10 percent, 12 percent, and 22 percent), which means the next dollar of your income above $60,000 will be taxed at 22 percent, which is thus your marginal tax rate.

After you determine your federal marginal tax rate, you'll need to add your marginal state tax rate to get your total combined marginal tax rate, including any deduction for state taxes.

Next, convert your pre-tax returns to after-tax returns for taxable bonds in order to see how they compare to tax-exempt (municipal) bonds. To do this, multiply the pre-tax return of a taxable bond by $(1-T)$, where T is your marginal tax rate.

For example, let's assume you're a taxable investor with a total tax rate of 40 percent, including federal and state income tax. If we take the pre-tax yield of 5.0 percent and multiply that by 0.60 $(1-0.40)$, we end up with a 3 percent after-tax yield, as seen in the table below. We can then compare taxable bonds to municipal bonds based on their after-tax yields, which shows us that in this case, the municipal bond has a higher yield.

Table 19. Taxable vs. Tax-Exempt Bond Yields

	Taxable Bond	Tax-Exempt Bond (Municipal)*
Pre-Tax Yield	5.0%	4.0%
1−Marginal Tax Rate (1−0.40=0.60)	60%	N/A
After-Tax Yield	3.0%	4.0%

*Assumes you pay no state income tax on this exempt bond offering.

In example 2 from the previous section (see table 18), the total allocation to bonds needs to be 30 percent total, with 20 percent in a tax-exempt account and 10 percent in a taxable account. For your taxable 10% bond portion, if your tax bracket is low enough that the after-tax return for taxable bonds is higher than the after-tax return for municipal bonds, then put that 10 percent in taxable bonds. If your tax bracket is high enough that it makes the after-tax returns for municipal bonds more attractive, like in the example above, then put the 10 percent in the taxable account in municipal bonds instead.

Do-It-Yourself Step #6: Deciding Whether to Include Impact Investing

Many investors increasingly want their portfolios to reflect their values. This is often referred to as impact investing, socially responsible investing (SRI), sustainable investing, or environmental, social, governance (ESG) investing. I'll use the latter term here.

You can implement ESG investing through a number of means, including negative screening ("I don't want to own any coal companies") or positive screening ("I want to overweight clean energy companies"). It can also incorporate, for stocks, ESG proxy voting or shareholder engagement.

In terms of the issues addressed, this type of investing can focus narrowly on one ESG issue or motivation—such as wanting to avoid tobacco companies—or it can incorporate a broad range of ESG issues simultaneously, like screening for the environment, social justice, and good corporate governance.

Those without much to invest can access ESG through mutual funds, while the very wealthy can invest through complex partnerships, like those found in sustainable forestry. Investors can also access ESG strategies across asset classes. For publicly traded stocks, ESG offers lots of different choices. For bonds and cash, it's a little harder to find ESG strategies, but they exist. For private equity (usually available only to the very wealthy), investors have a wide range of choices, and more limited choices for real assets. Finally, ESG stock investors can find strategies delivered through both expensive active management and low-cost indexing.

The Dangers of Self-Serving Bias in ESG Investing

Great opportunities exist if you want to incorporate ESG issues into your portfolio, but, as you can guess by now, you'll need to watch out for the industry's biases as well as your own, the same as for conventional investing.

Our own bias here comes back to what social psychologist Jonathan Haidt explains in his book *The Happiness Hypothesis* about how the neocortex comes up with rationalizations to justify and validate emotion-driven and subconscious desires.

When ESG investors believe passionately in their values, their fervor easily leads to the distorted view that ESG strategies will *necessarily* provide market-beating returns for stocks. I've been assured, in emphatic terms, by ESG advocates that you can bank on such strategies outperforming the stock market—even in the absence of any research evidence supporting that view. Our minds also already tend to seek out only confirming data as a general rule (confirmation bias), and with ESG investors, sometimes the requirement for *any* data or evidence gets waived entirely.

When it comes to the biases of investment managers, again, the profit incentive can interfere with their best advice for you as a consumer. For active managers, the increased demand for ESG investment strategies has proved a godsend, especially when catering (or pandering) to passionate ESG investors who are willing to pay much higher fees to implement ESG investments. Furthermore, the investment industry, much of which scornfully dismissed ESG until recently, now salivates at the prospect of selling ESG even when the actual environmental, social, or governance benefits may not amount to much.

Many companies wrap their bad behavior in lofty ESG terms even when they haven't actually changed much, like energy companies claiming they've "seen the light" when it comes to their role in pollution, when in fact, their public relations arm simply touts whatever tiny steps they've taken as a way to distract the public from the problem. This is known as *greenwashing* in the corporate world, and investment firms are also guilty of it. In fact, the Securities and Exchange Commission issued a warning in April 2021 that they had "observed unsubstantiated or otherwise potentially misleading claims regarding ESG investing in a variety of contexts."[52]

Similarly, the food industry has pounced on the opportunity to cater to a perceived demand for healthier eating, but of course they benefit from fooling consumers by marketing unhealthy foods as healthy options. Food marketers understood this dynamic well when they began to sell yogurt to parents by packing it with sugar to ensure the kids will like it. (I've heard skeptics describe yogurt targeted at children as a "sugar delivery mechanism" similar to how cigarettes have been designed as "nicotine delivery mechanisms.")

The investment industry has observed a jump in demand for ESG, and now the industry offers all kinds of ESG strategies—whether or not they actually provide much or any impact. To be fair to the industry, ESG comprises many belief systems, and the lack of clear definition makes it harder to determine an offering's quality, both from an investment perspective and in terms of its ESG impact.

As a savvy investor, you need to remain on guard about how the industry might offer you either excellent ESG opportunities or snake oil. What makes this challenging is that wealth or asset managers can provide good opportunities or awful ones—while many investment managers will offer high-cost ways to invest in ESG values in a way that enriches themselves, others may provide excellent ways to combine ESG values with good investment management.

If you want to incorporate ESG values into your portfolio, you'll need to bring the same wariness to your analysis that you do for non-ESG investing. First, focus on the fees, and ask yourself if you have to pay a lot of extra money just to incorporate your values. Many low-cost index strategies provide ESG values, so default to those as you investigate your choices. Also, be sure that anyone selling you ESG isn't promising market-beating returns.

And finally, if I seem hostile to ESG investing, it's actually the contrary: I've published papers proving that investors don't have to give up returns as long as they use reasonable ESG screens.[53]

Do-It-Yourself Step #7:
Ongoing Portfolio Management

Most investment how-to books end right after you've read about the recommended portfolio, without addressing market conditions. As you can see in this table, my recommendations across different market conditions are simple (and only slightly tongue-in-cheek), assuming you've already implemented a good passive asset allocation for your situation.

Table 20. Recommended Responses to Different Market Conditions

Market Condition	Recommended Action
Market has been climbing. You feel it may be dangerously high, or you worry you'll miss out on further growth.	Sit tight and do nothing.
Market has been falling. You're worried it will keep dropping.	Sit tight and do nothing.
Market seems to be without direction, careening higher, then lower.	Sit tight and do nothing.

Over time, however, market movements may put your target allocation and your actual portfolio out of whack. Let's assume you're aiming for a 70 percent risky/30 percent safer allocation, but a big drop in the stock market means you're down to 60 percent risky/40 percent safer. This means that when you need to add cash, you should direct it to the risky bucket to get its proportion back up toward 70 percent. If you need to withdraw cash, take it from the safer bucket since it's now too high.

Some advisors recommend tight bands on asset allocation, rebalancing whenever your portfolio strays more than, say, 5 percent from your target. I prefer a looser approach, allowing for fluctuations of 10 percent or more off-target. While the math shows the superiority behind the recommendations for tight bands, from a behavioral perspective, in the middle of a big decline, it's one thing to ask people not to sell their risky assets, but it's an even taller request to ask them to rebalance by selling their safer assets right when their anxiety is at its highest.

Chapter 10

How to Hire a Wealth Manager

MAYBE THE DIY ROUTE just doesn't work for you, or the services you need support hiring someone. It's a perfectly valid decision to bring on a wealth manager, as long as you're making it with your eyes wide open.

Start this process by identifying the useful services from chapter 8 that you think you'll need. They are financial planning, one-off financial decisions, trading and reporting (hassle reduction), hand-holding, initial asset allocation, education on more obscure investment concepts or techniques, and taxes. I recommend flipping back to chapter 8 now to refresh your memory and make a list of any services you may want help with.

There are four main aspects to hiring a wealth manager: choosing a human or *robo* advisor, deciding how you want to pay, vetting and interviewing potential managers (if you decide to go the human route), and finding the right balance of rapport and investment advice. Let's examine each in detail.

Choosing between a Human and a Robot

Robo (which stands for robot or robotic) advisors have become a popular option for today's investors, because they manage a portfolio automatically without a human picking stocks or adjusting asset allocation. When robos first became popular, they generated a lot of excitement but also anxiety among wealth advisors. The latter arose from two serious misconceptions.

The first misconception was that robo advisors were going to put traditional wealth advisors out of business. This proved false when investors failed to move en masse to automated portfolio management as a substitute for any human interaction. In general, investors with larger balances of, say, a million dollars or more still want to interact with a human being.

The second misconception was that businesses offering only robo advice would replace traditional wealth advisory firms. This was similar to the fears in the late 1990s that Internet banking would put traditional banks out of business, when of course that's not what happened; instead, the big banks were simply forced to start offering online banking. Similarly, Vanguard, Schwab, Fidelity, and others began offering their own robo advisors, much to the disappointment of the robo-only firms who were hoping to replace them.

Robo advisors have pulled back the curtain on how simple asset allocation can be—they highlight just how easy it is to automate this process. They're usually low cost, and they often offer better tax efficiency. Consumers benefit from their emphasis on fees and taxes, as these are the parts of investing that can actually be controlled.

However, while robo advisors can be a great choice, solutions limited to robotic rebalancing with no human contact can fall short on many of the other useful services wealth advisors provide, such as hand-holding during a crisis, education, and help with one-off financial decisions. This is why many robo services now offer access to a human advisor, although there is debate as to how beneficial the human advisory component can actually be with such platforms since the relationship isn't as solid as with a traditional wealth manager.

Although robos are inexpensive compared to live advisors, they're still more expensive than pre-packaged mutual funds that automatically rebalance for you, such as Vanguard's Target Retirement funds. Even Vanguard's robo service incurs an unnecessary cost if all you need is one of their Target Retirement funds. This tension between simplicity (often the best choice for investors, but not always) and an extra layer of service (often best for the investment industry, but sometimes helpful for you too) remains a challenge.

The bottom line? If you just want the hassle reduction of automated rebalancing and the initial setting up of an asset allocation, robos can offer a great way to get low-cost, simple portfolios. If you want that human touch, however, robos may not provide a satisfying solution.

If you do pick a robo advisor, make sure you're only paying for what you need. If you find asset allocation and rebalancing daunting enough that you're willing to pay, say, 0.30 percent of your portfolio per year, that's an acceptable choice. Remember, the same logic applies to robo and human advisors alike: you want the simple Broccoli portfolio of Transparent Investing, not the complicated, time-consuming Chocolate Cake portfolio.

Deciding How to Pay for Investment Advice

Maybe you've concluded that a robo advisor isn't the best solution for you, or maybe you're still open to it but are exploring your options. Either way, now it's time to decide how you want to pay for investment advice.

Over the period from 1990 to 2020, the investment industry has undergone a dramatic shift from the commissions model to the assets under management model, which is now the norm. However, some wealth managers still get paid by commission, and it's uncommon for these advisors to emphasize low-cost index funds. This goes back to the presumption that a good portfolio should be complicated, and that shrewd investing means seeing a lot of activity (i.e., that you should see your manager "doing something"). If you're paying commissions based on the hope that your wealth manager will beat the market, you should look for another manager.

When paying a percentage of your assets under management (AUM), you can receive either great value or pay way too much, mainly because the AUM model often bundles together both useful and suspect services. For example, if you just want help setting up your initial asset allocation, the ongoing, bundled nature of the AUM model means you pay annually for what was a one-time service. On the other hand, assessing whether this ongoing fee is worthwhile can play out in either direction: some clients don't think they need the additional bundled services they're paying for and then they do, while other clients think they'll use those extra services and then they don't.

You may also encounter wealth managers who charge based on AUM but require a higher minimum portfolio size than what you can invest. If this is the case, you'll find yourself limited to commissions, an hourly rate, or a robo advisor.

The final payment method is the hourly rate or retainer. The hourly option remains uncommon, even though it's attractive for the DIY investor with a simple portfolio of index funds. (If you're comfortable executing these transactions yourself and only want a wealth manager to monitor the portfolio, for example, this could mean paying for as little as an hour or two of their time every couple of years.)

If you choose hourly, remember that, like all the ways of paying for advice, it comes with its advantages and disadvantages depending on which services you need. With the AUM model, you're paying for your advisor to be readily available to help with any issues that arise. From a behavioral standpoint, therefore, you're more likely to contact them and ask for their advice. If you're paying hourly, on the other hand, it may seem too expensive to call your advisor even though you may benefit from their advice. Furthermore, it can be harder to build trust and rapport with an advisor who's paid hourly.

Finding investment advisors who charge hourly can also prove challenging. Advisors make more money through the AUM approach, so they don't tend to offer or encourage hourly fees. Still, from a cost perspective, hourly does provide one of the best ways to avoid paying for services you don't need or want. Beyond hourly, paying a retainer fee not tied to assets has become more popular with some wealth advisors.

It can be a challenge to find wealth managers who provide the useful (versus suspect) services without charging you unreasonably high fees. Unfortunately, the industry's compensation structure makes it difficult to implement Broccoli-focused investing because Chocolate Cake pays the experts better. I've advised many friends who've lamented that they just need one-off advice for specific situations, but they can't seem to find an honest advisor who will provide only that one useful service without managing their entire portfolio.

You may find yourself in a similar situation in which you want a client–advisor relationship that provides what you need, but the choices remain to either do it all yourself or pay high fees for services that don't provide value on average. Your choice, then, may be to reexamine whether you can tolerate doing it all yourself or bite the bullet and pay for what you don't really need.

Vetting and Interviewing Potential Managers

I often read articles on how to pick an advisor, and I almost always find that the general advice misses the main point, which is to find an advisor who will sell you only on the things that can be controlled, not on the fantasy of what can't be.

The following table shows the traditional (Chocolate Cake mindset) approach to the five main aspects of vetting and interviewing a wealth manager—referrals, credentials, fees, active versus passive, and taxes—compared to the Transparent Investing (Broccoli mindset) approach.

Table 21. Vetting Potential Managers: Chocolate Cake vs. Broccoli

	Traditional Approach (Chocolate Cake mindset)	Challenges of the Traditional Approach	Transparent Investing Approach (Broccoli mindset)
Referrals	Ask family or friends how well they like their advisors.	Often, family or friends simply describe how warm the relationship is, irrespective of the price or quality of investment strategies.	Ask friends and family if their advisors use indexing or have them in active strategies that rely on outperforming the market.
Credentials	Check out the credentials of advisors, like Certified Financial Planner or Chartered Financial Analyst.	Credentials and academic degrees signal a certain level of training and knowledge, but they don't guarantee ethics and a focus on selling only what adds value.	Looking at credentials can be helpful, but these are less important than an advisor's honesty about what they can and can't do.
Fees	Understand fees, but don't just go with the lowest one.	Low fees don't guarantee good investment advice, but high fees, especially the hidden variety, strongly signal bad value.	Honest fees are more important than low fees, but keep in mind that most high fees are from advisory firms that aren't upfront about their lack of ability with a crystal ball.

Active vs. Passive	Find the wizard who will beat the market.	The odds are heavily stacked against the ability to time or beat the market.	Find a wealth manager who is honest about what value they can add.
Taxes	Taxes are an afterthought, if addressed at all.	Taxes can lower your returns even more than high fees.	Be sure that your wealth manager treats your taxable and tax-deferred accounts differently and acknowledges the tax drag from active.

Below are some interview questions to use as you evaluate whether a particular wealth manager fits your needs.

You'll see that these questions focus first on the easiest component to control: how much you're paying in fees. For this, remember that you'll need to add up the different layers of fees (direct fees paid to the wealth manager, fees for the asset managers, and transaction costs) and focus on what we'll call the "all-in" fees.

As a follow-up to their explanation on fees, ask the wealth manager where they believe they add value, especially when it comes to the useful services you need. The more they emphasize the picking of active asset managers or market timing, the warier you should be of their pitch. Some wealth managers propose a mixture of indexing and active management, which is certainly preferable to all active, but you still need to hear why they expect their performance will beat the dismal performance of an industry that's failed to beat the market on average.

Questions to Ask Potential Wealth Managers

1. What are the total fees I'll be paying? What's the breakdown between the fees I pay to you, the fees I pay the asset managers you select, and transaction or other implicit costs? How are your advisors compensated? (The question about advisor compensation may be appropriate only for larger firms.)

2. Which services do you provide, and which of these do you think you excel at? (When you ask this, focus on the services you've already determined you need.)

3. What's your philosophy on active management? If you do focus on active, why do you believe your predictions of the future will prove superior to so much documented research showing the failure to beat the market? Do you measure your asset managers' performance *after* you recommend them to a client, or do you only look at their performance *before* you make the recommendation? (The more a wealth manager focuses on the historical performance of the strategies they're selling you, the bigger the red flag.)

4. What are your credentials and areas of specialization?

5. Do you offer all the services I need? Do you offer more services than I need? Can I get services separately, or do you offer only one packaged version?

6. Do you address my non-investment needs, like insurance and trust services? If not, how do you interact with the other experts in my financial life, including those helping me with insurance, taxes, legal needs, and estate planning? What's your philosophy on bundling these services together versus combining separate providers? (As a consumer, you're often better off unbundling combined services because it's the only way you can accurately assess the cost of each service you're buying.)

When interviewing a prospective wealth advisor, it helps to focus on the services you've actually determined you need rather than the potential chocolate cake they may entice you with. Throughout their pitch, keep in mind the difference between useful and suspect services (it can help to review chapter 8 before an interview). Beware of wealth managers who won't offer you the useful services unless you pay them for their efforts to beat the market.

Also, while you should seek out ethical wealth managers who tell you the truth and provide only useful services, unfortunately, high ethics don't necessarily guarantee you'll get a smart and effective advisor. Similarly, finding a smart advisor doesn't mean your interests will come first. The ideal advisor will combine high ethics with investment savvy and smarts.

Finding the Right Balance between Rapport and Solid Investment Advice

As you interview wealth managers, it's important to remember that while personal rapport and a warm bond can make you feel good about the advisor, these aren't enough to constitute a relationship that's truly beneficial to you as the client. In fact, a warm connection can be used to distract you from useless high fees or ineffective active strategies due to our old friend information asymmetry. While warmth can make the advisor–client relationship feel good, you want to avoid paying for friendship instead of service (a trap that even the wealthiest investors fall into).

A warm bond can help when an advisor plays the role of therapist, providing soothing comfort in turbulent markets, for instance. During these times, advisors try their best to talk clients down from the ledge and keep them from doing foolish things like selling at the bottom of a bear market. However, as with much of investing, the trick is finding the right balance—in this case, the balance between the real benefits of personal rapport and warmth and the hard facts of investment performance and fees.

Here's a quick test. Using the table below, which advisor would you choose?

Table 22. Comparison of Management Styles

	Manager 1	Manager 2
Warmth of Relationship	Warm bond, maybe going back many years, based on genuine rapport and affection.	Professional and courteous, but without a strong personal connection.
Investment Advice	Advice focused on active management—basically offering you expensive chocolate cake that may not prove ideal for your financial health.	Advice without conflict of interest that's focused on a simple, sustainable portfolio reflecting actual historical research.

Yes, it's a trick question, as I'm hoping you'll pick Manager 2 since that relationship will mean a higher level of wealth for you at the end of the day.

Ideally, an advisor provides emotional support that helps the client get through difficult issues while also charging reasonable fees and picking reliable, low-cost investment strategies like indexing. I don't discount the value added by having a strong rapport with your advisor; I'm just saying you're probably in trouble if it's the only benefit of your relationship.

Picking an advisor when you aren't an expert in investing can seem like a daunting experience; unfortunately, this is the reality of information asymmetry. However, now that you know more about fees, what services you truly need, and some sense of what makes for a beneficial advisor, hopefully the process will be easier.

Conclusion

MANY SELF-HELP BOOKS tell us that, if only we use their new and exciting methods, it's actually easy to lose weight, build a more lucrative career, or achieve spiritual breakthroughs. After all, if these books told the truth about how much discipline these behavioral changes actually take, they wouldn't sell as many copies. And like any other expert, I can fall into the blind spot of presuming it's easier to do all this strategizing and investing because it's something I do every day.

As humans, when we understand something conceptually (thanks, neocortex) and identify it as a goal, we expect our actual behavior (hello again, amygdala) to adapt quickly to match. And while the better investment choices shown in this book are easy to understand conceptually (build a simple portfolio of index funds that reflects the right asset allocation and don't fiddle with it very often), changing our behavior and thinking regarding investing may present a challenge.

For example, I recently helped a family friend I've known for over fifty years build a portfolio for the first time in her life. She told me how bothered she felt that she'd never taken the steps to think about her financial future comprehensively. I've encountered this kind of guilt before, when investors blame themselves for not having addressed an important issue in their lives. In my friend's case, her anxiety came from not knowing where to start and feeling intimidated by the industry. I suggested that she read an earlier version of the material in this book as a first step. Soon after, she told me that my written summary had made her anxiety disappear since she now at least understood how the game worked.

When she told me this, I realized it represented the most important goal for me in writing this book: that investors feel less intimidated by the entire process. I hope that, after reading this, you also feel less apprehensive and more confident about both what makes you tick financially as well as how the investment profession operates.

Counterarguments

As you read this book, some counterarguments to my recommendation to choose passive investing may have popped into your mind. Here are the most common counterarguments I hear, along with my final takeaways for each.

1. All the research you cite may be valid, but I have this friend or relative who's had great success with active investing.

Just because I've presented compelling research that professional investors don't beat or time the market after fees on average doesn't mean there aren't individuals, professional or not, who do earn higher returns than the market. I'm claiming that the odds are heavily stacked against you, not that it's impossible—your friend or relative might have done better than the odds suggest, but one anecdote doesn't prove the averages are wrong.

It's easy to find exciting stories of success in the investment world, but your own investments should reflect performance reality. Remember too that no one tends to brag about their lack of investment success, i.e., you're hearing about only the most positive outcomes. I also bring a healthy dose of skepticism to these stories, since in my experience, people who claim to outperform aren't always measuring themselves against the right benchmarks.

For example, you might brag about having earned a 30 percent return last year in your stock portfolio, conveniently ignoring the fact that the entire stock market earned

31 percent during the same time period, meaning you did worse comparatively. I rarely encounter investment-prowess stories in which the actual data has been measured properly, especially when it comes to the actual returns that investors receive after fees and taxes.

I once worked with a client who hired our firm to manage a blend of stocks and bonds for a portion of his portfolio and hired another firm to manage just stocks for him. He told me we'd done well for him, but that the other firm had done much better during an up market—ignoring the fact that of course the other firm would do better in that situation, since they managed only the highest-returning portion of his portfolio (stocks). Ideally, he should have compared my firm's return to a blended benchmark of stocks and bonds (in the same proportion as our portion of his portfolio), and the other firm against solely a stock benchmark.

2. You're just saying that all active management is bad and should always be avoided.

I'm not saying active never works. I know some excellent and honorable wealth managers who focus on active management, and a few even have track records of beating the market after adjusting for risk. Instead, I'm simply saying that you should start with the data that show the industry's poor track record with active across time and across all active managers.

More importantly, I'm saying that the transparent investing approach represents a sound, prudent, and defensible way to invest based on passive asset allocation, passive security selection, and going for long periods without tweaking your portfolio. In other words, it's not that active is awful; it's that a simple indexing portfolio is so solid and wise. This is the reality that can threaten many active managers.

3. You're recommending that everyone should manage their own portfolio and not use professionals.

I've pointed out the ways wealth managers can add value depending on which services you need. Nonetheless, the industry is effectively lying when it tells potential clients that they should never try managing a portfolio on their own. When measured by average performance, especially after-tax, the research shows how ridiculous and self-serving this stance is.

If professionals want to argue with you that behavioral finance proves how dangerous our biases as investors can be to our wealth, they raise a valid point, but you can counter with the fact that behavioral analysis also shows how biased investment pros can be, since they benefit financially from selling you their services.

4. You're oversimplifying.

It is oversimplifying to claim that simple is always best, but it isn't oversimplifying to say that the industry often falls back on unnecessary complexity as a way to sell you services you may not need.

You may face situations so complex that professional advice is worth a lot. Nonetheless, you also face an industry that is, on the whole, desperate to persuade you that the best portfolios need to be complicated by nature, and that's a lot of self-serving rot.

The Challenge of Facing the Truth

Let's assume that—in spite of the counterarguments that may have come to mind as you read these pages—you've accepted the argument that your brain has evolved in ways that make you vulnerable to bad investment decisions.

While it's liberating to learn about our own biases, it's unpleasant to acknowledge that we have gaps in our thinking and behavior. Even though I'm constantly provided an endless stream of evidence highlighting my own biases, that knowledge doesn't always make it easier for me to acknowledge my blind spots. I have an ego just like everyone else, and it's painful when I catch myself making a motivated rationalization, for instance. However, understanding your own biases, such as the illusion of control, can help you avoid assuming there's a wizard out there who can predict the future.

Being clear about how you're wired to behave also means you can take a fresh look at the investment industry and see where, out of self-interest, it promises things it can't deliver. If you do decide to hire a wealth manager, you're now able to determine whether you're buying chocolate cake or broccoli. If you opt to manage your own portfolio, you know that the best default choice is a simple mix of low-cost index investments that you leave alone. You also know that while you do take on some hassle by managing your own portfolio, simple portfolios provide the extra advantage of requiring very little time to oversee.

The Utopian Version of the Investment Industry

For the sake of a thought experiment, let's take a brief look at the utopian paradise of an investment industry with no financial incentive to sell you expensive services. How would investment managers treat you if they were focused entirely on your needs?

First of all, we would act with great humility, viewing it as our job to explain just how limited our ability to predict the future is. Even if we wanted to push active, we would educate you on how stacked the odds are against both outperforming or timing the stock market (therefore recommending, as a default, passive asset allocation and passive security selection).

We would be honest about our services that add value and clearly state how much the research contradicts the notion of looking into a crystal ball. For taxable investors, we would treat the harm to wealth from taxes with the same seriousness we treat any other lowering of investment returns—in other words, we'd act as though *we* have to pay the taxes based on our choices.

In terms of how we get paid, we'd explain what you actually get for your money when you pay us as a percentage of assets. We'd offer you the choice of a fixed or hourly fee if that approach fits your needs better. We would be upfront whenever there is a conflict of interest, such as when selling you a certain product makes us more money than an alternative solution that still achieves your goal. We may still charge you significant amounts for our expertise, because the investment knowledge that actually matters takes years to develop, but our pricing and services would be far more transparent.

In the psychological realm, we would help you understand your own biases and the ways in which your brain is wired to make certain poor investment choices. We would help you understand how much of investing is behavioral, even as we help you understand the math part, which of course still matters. We'd be honest about our own biases as well, acknowledging our financial incentive to avoid discussing what the research has concluded about active management. We would also help you get past your own blind spots without capitalizing on them for monetary gain.

Just like in that scene in the *Wizard of Oz*, we'd strive to be good people by acting as teachers and guides rather than posing as wizards who promise something we can't deliver.

Back in the Real World

These utopian wealth managers do exist in the real world, but unfortunately, across the entire profession, they're not likely to be as upfront as you and I would both prefer. This just means that you'll have to push for transparency yourself as a wise consumer, by using the tools and techniques we've covered throughout these pages. By asking the right questions and figuring out whether you're being sold broccoli or chocolate cake, you can understand what a wealth manager can and can't provide.

While you do need to bring a certain level of wariness to your interaction with wealth managers or asset managers, remember the downside of too much cynicism. My goal is to make the investment world less intimidating, including your interactions with investment managers, but I don't want to make you so jaded that you assume there's no value to be gained from paying for advice.

Parting Words

My intention with this book is to provide at least some help to investors of all wealth levels. Much of my professional success came down to the hard work, cleverness, and ingenuity of a lot of people around me who sometimes made me look more competent as a CEO than my actual skills warranted. I also benefited from plenty of plain old good luck.

I hope this book has proved useful to you, even in a small way, since it feels good to have the opportunity to return the favor to a world that has been so generous to me.

A Letter to Readers

DEAR READER:

I hope you've found *Transparent Investing* to be helpful as you deal with your investments and how you interact with the investment industry.

As I have mentioned, I envision this book as a kind of "shot across the bow" in a Transparent Investing movement. I'm trying to encourage as many investors as possible to understand and act upon the concepts you've now read about. I'm hopeful that as consumers become more educated and put pressure on the financial industry, more advisors and firms will step up their efforts to be more transparent.

This book is key to spreading the word, and reviews are an essential part of any book's ability to reach readers. If you enjoyed the book, would you do me the personal favor of writing a review for it online such as at Amazon.com, Goodreads.com, or any other such site?

For the same reason, if you found it helpful, please mention it to your friends or colleagues. The more consumers we can educate about how investing really works, the more pressure can be brought to bear on increasing transparency across the industry.

Don't forget to visit my website, where you can grab a number of free and useful tools at:

patrickgeddes.co/transparent-investing

Joining my mailing list will further ensure you get notified of new content releases, upcoming online courses, and more. Please stay connected as we broaden the movement!

Acknowledgments

THIS BOOK WOULD never have come to fruition without the constant energy and dedication of Ally Machate, my editor, and her team at The Writer's Ally. Not only did she greatly improve the text and get me to focus more on the reader's experience, but she was also the one who provided the discipline so that it actually got written in the first place. Molly McCowan further improved the text, as I learned how helpful it can be to have a really smart line editor.

John Jennings provided some of the most detailed and helpful comments on the manuscript, including saving me from sounding foolish by including some psychological concepts now debunked. As CEO I was constantly getting credit for the work of others, and the preparation of this book provided further examples. The following readers all provided helpful suggestions and comments: Kirsten Meder, Heather Pelant, Christopher Dunham, Opa Hysea Wise, and Megan Rodkin. Farley Ziegler and Charles Cross both delivered not only worthwhile feedback, but also excitement around the importance of the message that buoyed me greatly.

Brian Lam provided some excellent additional research on academic work across a wide range of investment subjects.

Finally, I'd like to thank Paul Solli, the other cofounder of Aperio Group. While he wasn't involved directly in the writing or editing of this book, almost all of the content grew out of conversations over twenty-three years working closely together as we applied our analytic skills and ethical outrage to an industry too often interested in serving its own interests. Aperio Group would never have existed without Paul, so by extension neither would this book.

Of course, any errors or shortcomings remain entirely my own responsibility.

Glossary

12b-1 Fees	Ongoing expenses within a mutual fund charged to cover the cost of paying a broker or other distribution channel. Originally designed to allow brokers to sell load funds yet spread the charge over a longer period, typically five years. In other words, instead of charging a client 5 percent up front for the purchase of a fund, the client is charged 1 percent per year for five years.

Active Management	The opposite of passive, active management can apply to asset allocation or security selection. The former means trying to time the market, and the latter means trying to beat the market. Active managers claim to have foresight as to future stock returns, and for that promise they generally charge much higher fees.
Asset Allocation	The overall weighting of a portfolio in asset classes such as domestic stocks, international stocks, bonds, cash, and other asset classes. Getting the balance between the risky and safer buckets is the most critical decision for most investors.
Asset Manager	An investment professional or company who manages a particular asset class or combination of asset classes like stocks or bonds. Frequently asset managers specialize even within an asset class, e.g., international stocks, municipal bonds, private real estate partnerships, or lots of others.

Asset Class	Broad category of a certain type of investment. The simplest asset classes include publicly traded stocks, bonds, and cash. Additional asset classes include private equity, real assets (real estate and resources such as timber), hedge funds (often but not always categorized as a separate asset class), and other more specialized strategies.
Broadly Diversified Passive	A term to describe not just technically indexing, but indexing that covers very broad markets, like the entire US stock market or the entire world outside of the US. An index fund that invests only in Thai stocks is technically still an index fund, but it's not BDP. (Note: this is not a standard industry term, but rather my own.)
Closed End Fund	A mutual fund that trades on a stock exchange rather than being bought and sold directly by the fund. Closed end funds trade at premiums and discounts, i.e., amounts greater or less than the fund NAV.

Exchange Traded Fund (ETF)	Exchange Traded Fund is a type of open-end mutual fund that trades on a stock exchange, like a stock. Most ETFs are index funds, but there are a few active. The differences between an ETF and a traditional open-end fund are generally slight.
Expenses	Ongoing fees to pay for the management of an investment strategy.
Financial Planner	A type of advisor that helps with defining and assessing long-term goals. Sometimes a financial planner offers asset management and sometimes not. Investment advisors often provide some planning, so the labels aren't always clearly delineated.
Index	A combination of securities used to represent an entire market, e.g., S&P500.
Index Fund	A mutual fund that purchases all or the equivalent of all securities in an index, thus avoiding any research expenses and generally ensuring low turnover. The biggest index funds are quite inexpensive, though not all indexing is low-cost.

Investment Advisor	Can be used as a broad term like investment manager but can also refer to a wealth manager.
Investment Manager	A general term that can include wealth manager, asset manager, or other related professional or firm who provides services to investors.
Load	A sales charge paid to an advisor or broker in exchange for selecting a fund, paid either up front or on an ongoing basis through a 12b-1 fee.
Load Fund	A mutual fund that charges a load.
Market Capitalization	The total stock market value of a stock, calculated by multiplying the share price times the number of shares outstanding.

Money Market Fund	A type of account considered in the cash asset class, holding debt of less than one year in maturity. Money market mutual funds seek to maintain a stable price of $1 per share, though they're generally not guaranteed by the FDIC or the fund company. It's the safest among the main asset classes for short-term fluctuations, although it is vulnerable to inflation. Except for certain government funds, they're not guaranteed by the federal government. Available in either taxable or muni versions. A money market account at a bank also pays interest but is generally guaranteed up to a certain limit by the FDIC.
Muni Bond	A bond that pays interest exempt from federal tax. States often assess no state income tax on munis issued within the state. Taxable munis do exist but are not as prevalent as tax-exempt.

Net Asset Value (NAV)	Net Asset Value, the value of a share of a mutual fund, calculated by adding together the total market value of all securities held by the fund and dividing by the number of shares outstanding.
No-Load Fund	A mutual fund that charges no loads at all. Technically, a fund must charge no 12b-1 fees to qualify as a "pure" no-load.
Open End Fund	A mutual fund for which the fund company readily buys and sells shares directly. The amount of money invested can fluctuate as investors add to or subtract from their shares in the fund.
Operating Expense	The ongoing charge to pay the management and administrators of a mutual fund. Both load and no-load funds charge operating expenses.
Passive Investing	The opposite of active investing, passive can apply to either asset allocation (don't try to time the market) or to security selection (don't try to beat the market). Passive investing usually means the same thing as indexing, at least for security selection.

Real Estate Investment Trust (REIT)	Real Estate Investment Trust, a stock that comprises real estate holdings. REITs allow investors to own real estate indirectly.
Wealth Manager	An investment advisor who works directly with clients, generally providing overall portfolio construction, especially the asset allocation. A wealth manager often selects asset managers to deliver the different asset classes, but sometimes the roles are combined. Wealth managers can provide a lot of services beyond just managing a portfolio.

Research Notes
by Chapter

Introduction

On the inability of economic forecasters, see Commins.

For an excellent analysis of biases in forecasting the future, see Tetlock et al. Tetlock and Gardner describe in detail what makes good forecasters across a wide range of fields. While being smart and well-informed certainly helps, the authors found that the critical component in better prediction reflected how much each forecaster examined her or his own assumptions and biases underneath each decision. They never describe it as humility, but they provide a lot of evidence for how the best forecasters relentlessly critique their own assumptions when making decisions rather than the traditional "I just go with my gut." Sometimes gut-driven decisions work very well, but for forecasting accuracy, self-awareness improves decision-making according to their research. Their observations can also help focus you, as an investor, on the dangers of biases within your own mind and also in the minds of finance pros you may hire to help you with your portfolio.

For how the Bogleheads approach investing, see Larimore et al., where you'll find a lot of philosophical overlap with *Transparent Investing*.

Chapter 1: Emotions Count More than Math

For an excellent summary of the published research on behavioral finance up through 2008, see Pompian. He summarizes twenty well-researched biases, including the references to the original academic articles published on each bias. In later works, Pompian goes further by dividing his list of biases into two separate categories based on how a wealth advisor should address client biases: those that can be addressed cognitively versus those that can be addressed emotionally.

For an updated and detailed summary of the literature, see the references in Madaan et al., Kumar et al., or Singh et al.

For an entertaining history of some of the origins of behavioral economics, see Lewis. See also Ariely and both books by Kahneman.

Chapter 2: The Illusion of Control, or How Epictetus Would Choose a Broccoli Portfolio

In his work *The Enchiridion*, Epictetus claims that if you focus on the things outside of your control, "you will find fault with both gods and men."

Regarding gender bias, the academic article "Boys Will Be Boys" outlines the concept of how males on average have exhibited higher levels of inappropriate overconfidence in their abilities. As reported by Jeff Sommer in the *New York Times*, Vanguard has also found similar results after examining the data for millions of their own investors. In the same *NYT* article, the professor Brad Barber, who cowrote "Boys Will Be Boys," commented, "Short-term financial news often amounts to little more than meaningless 'noise' . . . Far more than women, men try to make sense out of this noise, and to no avail." Barber articulates the problem well, alluding to the evolutionary inclination to get so good at recognizing patterns that all of us (males in particular) tend to see them even where they don't exist.

For an excellent summary of how challenging it can prove to rid yourself of bias, see Galef. She provides helpful tips on how to avoid motivated thinking.

For more detail on the impact of fees on stock investing, see the Research Notes section for chapter 6 on the industry's track record.

Chapter 4: The Biases and Motivations of Investment Managers

On social media and its impact on the brain, see Haynes and Parkin.

Regarding cognitive dissonance, the term was coined by psychologist Leon Festinger in the 1950s. In their book *When Prophecy Fails*, a classic work of social psychology published in 1956, Festinger and his coauthors describe the study of a small UFO religion near Chicago called the Seekers that believed in an imminent apocalypse and of the group's coping mechanisms after the event did not occur. Festinger's theory of cognitive dissonance can account for the psychological consequences of disconfirmed expectations. For investors the lesson reinforces the wariness anyone should bring to forecasting the market. In addition, it highlights how, when confronted with contradictory evidence, our brains grasp desperately for some explanation that preserves our belief system, however inconsistent with the facts. I would argue that same clinging to beliefs shows up when the investment industry continues to ask investors to have faith in their professionals' ability to time and beat the market. In this case, however, the bias that makes investment advisors cling to beliefs that don't reflect well-researched data comes not from religious passion but rather from old-fashioned economic self-interest.

For more detail on confirmation bias, see Gilovich. In *How We Know What Isn't So*, he provides an excellent summary of the research on how we look for only one bit of evidence to support or dismiss a strongly held belief, even if the preponderance of evidence or research shows the opposite.

For further research on confirmation bias, see Cheng.

On how our brains fabricate explanations not grounded in observation or other reality solely to justify our preferences, see Haidt. For more detail, see descriptions of the work by Michael Gazzaniga in Gazzaniga and Smith. Gazzaniga tested subjects who, for controlling seizures, had gone through an operation to sever the corpus callosum, which connects the left and right hemispheres of the brain. In the test, Gazzaniga would show pictures separately to each side of the brain, since the left eye is "controlled" by the right side of the brain and the right eye by the left side of the brain. One subject was shown a chicken's foot to the left side of the brain and a winter scene to the right. Afterward, when back in stereoscopic mode, the subject correctly picked from a selection of images the two that matched what had been shown to each side separately, a chicken's head for the left side and a shovel to go with the winter scene viewed by only the right side. The left side, since it was isolated from the right brain, had no idea that the right brain had picked a shovel because of the presence of snow. However, when asked why he had picked the picture of a shovel, the subject completely made up out of thin air a logical sounding explanation by saying, "Oh, that's simple. . . . The chicken claw goes with the chicken and you need a shovel to clean out the chicken shed." Source: Smith.

Why does that research matter in the investment world? I argue throughout this book that both investors and investment managers create fabricated narratives to support or justify their beliefs or inclinations, a tendency we all exhibit at one time or another. A key to excellent investing lies in the ability to 1) catch yourself when you start seeing nonexistent patterns in random data or spinning a narrative that's not grounded in data but makes you feel better nonetheless, and 2) notice when an investment manager trying to sell you expertise does the same thing in the effort to assuage your anxiety about how random financial markets can be. Your anxiety over the unpredictable nature of markets reflects a normal human concern for the future, but deciding that you or a hired advisor brings a wizard's skill in reading a crystal ball as a way to lower that anxiety can lead to bad investment choices and paying too much in fees for dubious promises to time or beat financial markets.

Analogous to how economic self-interest distorts our reasoning, research has shown that our political beliefs (from either side of the spectrum) also bias how we analyze data. See Mooney's article "Science Confirms: Politics Wrecks Your Ability to Do Math," and Kahan et al. Kahan and colleagues found that a certain proportion of subjects showed a skill at spotting a subtle statistical distortion when looking at data on a neutral topic like the medical benefits of skin cream. However, when the exact same data set got presented in the context of a hot-button political issue, people failed to see the flaw when it went against their own political view, though they could still see the fallacy when it applied to the opposing side. I would argue that investment managers seeking to protect both their income streams and self-images, like all humans, tend to ignore data that might threaten either.

For details on the quotation from Galileo, see Favaro.

Chapter 5: How Investment Managers Get Paid

For average expense ratios, see the Morningstar Manager Research. The Morningstar report presents data in two ways, one that's called *equal-weighted*, which simply reflects the average for every mutual fund in a category. That methodology would support my criticism of high fees much more strongly, but it's not as accurate as the other way they present the data, defined as *dollar-weighted*. The latter method shows the average fee weighted by how much money investors have placed in various funds, which means it emphasizes the big funds that hold the vast majority of assets, ignoring small funds that might happen to have high fees but aren't as relevant. I'd consider it potentially biased to show the equal-weighted version, and thus I want to minimize potentially valid criticism of cherry-picking.

That's why the dollar-weighted data reflect actual investor experience better.

Additional detail can be found in Thune; for difference between active and passive, see Krikorian.

Chapter 6, The Industry's Track Record

Summarizing all the research on active management can prove challenging, as there's no individual authoritative article or book that single-handedly proves the superiority of passive, just an overwhelming preponderance from many sources. In addition, the measurement methodology and choice of time horizon can also confuse the issue, sometimes to the benefit of those seeking to emphasize the rare but still present times when active does well compared to passive.

Research on Security Selection

Before presenting the research findings, it's helpful to identify some important methodological issues that arise when analyzing active security selection. The research results make more sense once the following issues have been made clear.

1. Focus on long-term returns

The debate on passive versus active should reflect long-term holding periods, as that reflects the time horizon of most individual investors. Of course shorter time horizons mean a different asset allocation may be appropriate, but data from periods of ten years or longer offer superior insight into your choices for yourself over such a time horizon. Looking at short-term outperformance implies you might be able to constantly readjust by picking the next short-term asset managers who will outperform, a very unlikely prospect. Thus, in the research supporting how passive should be virtually every investor's default, I focus on historical time horizons of ten years or longer.

2. Survivorship bias

When historical performance gets displayed by the press or the investment industry, it usually appears reflecting the simple approach of showing, say for mutual funds, all the funds in a particular category with ten-year track records. The flaw in that approach lies in the fact that many funds may have had such bad performance that they had to be closed or folded into other funds, and those get left out unless you control for that problem. Thus the best data reflects going back in time and including the worst performers to avoid what is known as survivorship bias.

3. Weight by dollars

To reflect accurately the average return, historical data should be weighted by the dollars in each investment strategy. That way, if you have one huge pool of assets, it counts a lot more than smaller ones since that represents the vote by dollars of investors.

4.   You can't invest in a benchmark

Almost all the research compares active managers to benchmarks, which of course aren't actually investment vehicles in which you can invest directly. However, you can invest in index funds with very low costs to capture virtually all categories. For example, Fidelity offers a Total Market Index Fund for the whole US stock market for a fee of 0.015 percent, which represents such a tiny cost that it wouldn't affect the performance data much. Technically the 87 percent of funds failing to beat a benchmark from the SPIVA study discussed below would be very slightly changed to a lower percentage were you to compare the historical performance of active funds to, say, a low-cost fund like Fidelity's. However, at a cost that low, such an adjustment doesn't save active management from having dismally failed investors while at the same time generating enormous profit for the industry.

Starting with the most straightforward data, for all US equity funds over a fifteen-year history ending in the middle of 2020, 87 percent of those funds failed to perform better than their benchmarks, according to the SPIVA US Scorecard from

S&P Dow Jones. That failure of active managers to beat a simple benchmark has been fairly consistent over the fifty years from 1970 to 2020.

For a good summary of the literature through 2006, see Holmes, especially for her excellent bibliography. A more recent literature summary can be found in Pace et al.

Vanguard's research group has also published corroborating evidence (see Rowley et al). While I advise wariness regarding research sourced from investment firms, Vanguard brings a higher level of credibility than most companies. Though they certainly have a vested interest in proving the benefits of indexing, I trust their research more than the findings from many firms since Vanguard's mutual funds are effectively co-ops, where the funds' investors, not Vanguard, own the fund. That structure doesn't guarantee that Vanguard will always publish only unbiased research, but it significantly lowers the likelihood of their publishing distortions of the data to justify higher fees when compared to for-profit investment firms.

In Rowley et al., "The Case for Low-Cost Index-Fund Investing," they present compelling evidence on many fronts. First they show how much survivorship bias distorts returns and how, for good unbiased data, you should believe only data sources that correct for that issue. Second, they highlight how much high fees correlate with poor investment performance.

Third, they provide powerful evidence of the dangers of picking winners based on historical performance. Many wealth managers may admit that the average active asset manager may not have beaten the appropriate benchmark over, say, the trailing five years before they're picking one for you. However, they'll frequently insist that their skills at picking consistent winners will prove their prowess at selecting in advance the strategies that will outperform. Unfortunately for that narrative, Vanguard's research shows how, when you look back over five years at performance of various categories of stock mutual funds, the ones that did outperform in the previous five years show up in the subsequent five years as fairly randomly distributed across good, middle, and poor performance. In other words, beating the market historically doesn't provide predictive power for doing so in the future. One consistent result remains, though, reflecting the fact that over the subsequent five years after selection, many funds, including the best performers, get liquidated or merged into other funds, thus proving again the need to control for survivorship bias.

Though it's out of date, in one of the best works of academic research, Carhart found in his 1997 paper that 80 to 90 percent of domestic active managers do not outperform the index. He found some limited consistency among the very worst and the very best. Carhart's work showed the benefit of controlling for survivorship bias as well as style, e.g., the distinction between what's often called value and growth investing or the one between large- and small-company stocks.

For evidence that the failure of active management has a long history, for time periods from before 2000, see Elton et al., Grinblatt et al., Goetzmann et al., Droms et al., and Malkiel.

Research on Active Asset Allocation (Market Timing)

As with security selection, a significant preponderance of research shows that investment managers fail in their efforts to time the market, defined here as active asset allocation.

Focusing instead on pension funds, Andonov et al. find that "larger pension funds would have done better if they invested more in passive mandates without frequent rebalancing across asset classes."

For hedge funds, Kang found that fund managers have "no timing skills."

Comer et al. found no evidence of market timing, although they did find some evidence of active asset allocation providing better downside protection than expected.

When studying UK pensions, Blake et al. found "uniformly poor market-timing performance." Speculating on the motivation of professionals that oversee institutional investment pools, the authors suggest the possible explanation that "plan sponsors or corporate treasury departments can justify their empires only if they engage in active management to some extent."

The research on both security selection and market timing strongly supports the superiority of passive approaches to each.

I'd argue that no serious debate exists within academic research about whether or not average investment managers can time or beat the stock market successfully. However, examples of managers who can outperform in both still exist, meaning valid debate may still exist as to whether such outperformance can remain predictable enough to be attributed to skill rather than luck. For the vast majority of investors, though, their financial well-being will end up better with simple buy-and-hold approaches using indexing. Thus the possibility of outperformance still exists, but it remains a poor bet, with the odds heavily stacked against anyone succeeding.

Chapter 7, Index Investing

On the flow of assets from active management to passive, see Gittelsohn and Segal.

Chapter 9, How to Do It Yourself

On after-tax risk analysis, see Geddes et al. (2015).

Notes

1. In fact, it's an oversimplification to describe the amygdala as the sole source of emotions like fear, but for purposes of discussion, it makes it easier to juxtapose the amygdala as the origin of the fight or flight response versus the neocortex as the place where analytic thinking occurs, even if the reality is more complicated.
2. Housel, 57–67.
3. Buffett.
4. Robbins.
5. For an excellent summary, see Pompian.
6. Epictetus.
7. From theologian Reinhold Niebuhr, although the exact date and source remain imprecise. For a history

of the prayer, see Shapiro.

8. University of Birmingham.

9. See Cheng, Madaan, Pompian 111–118, Singh.

10. Barber et al.

11. Wright et al. The article specifically states that when women were given testosterone, they found evidence of overconfidence in a social setting as an "enhanced weighting of one's own relative to another's evidence."

12. Nadler et al. For a summary of research on testosterone, see also Huston.

13. Graham, 8.

14. After I had come up with the chocolate cake versus broccoli analogy, I began researching to make sure no one else had used that comparison previously. To my chagrin, I did find the chocolate cake and broccoli example in an investment book from 1998, *The Roaring 2000s*, by Harry S. Dent, Jr. Dent recommends a very different investment philosophy from the one in this book, but it proved another excellent lesson in humility to learn I hadn't been the first one to come up with the pairing of chocolate cake and broccoli!

15. Kinnel.

16. Duke.

17. Ennis, "Institutional Investment Strategy and Manager Choice: A Critique."

18. http://sitn.hms.harvard.edu/flash/2018/
dopamine-smartphones-battle-time/.

19. Parkin.

20. Pompian, 83–93.

21. Moser. See also Festinger.

22. Haidt.

23. Gilovich, 75–88.

24. Favaro.

25. Sinclair, 109.

26. Kinnel.

27. Morningstar.

28. Liu.

29. Businesswire.

30. Kinnel.

31. Liu.

32. Ennis "Endowment Performance."

33. Sommer.

34. Swedroe, 2013, 35–38.

35. Clare et al.

36. Ennis Knupp.

37. Ellis, 27.

38. Andonov et al.

39. Ferri, 39–48.

40. McCullough.

41. Johnson.

42. As of July 13, 2020.

43. Many index providers go even further by taking the cap-weighted proportion and adjusting it for the actual shares traded in the stock market. For example, a publicly traded stock may have a significant market cap, but if a lot of that stock is owned by, say, a founder who doesn't trade those shares, then for the weight in the index an adjustment is made to reflect "market float," i.e., the number of shares available, not including those owned by the founder. Float-adjustments are perfectly appropriate as a way to modify strict cap-weighted indexes.

44. Segal.

45. For an excellent illustrative story, see Swedroe, 2020.

46. Note that when I caution investors to be highly wary of annuities, I'm speaking skeptically about annuities as a vehicle for accumulating wealth. That's a separate question from what I'll call *annuitizing*, which here we'll define as converting a pool of wealth into an income stream payable regularly over the remaining part of your lifetime or of the combined lifetimes of you and a spouse, for example. Annuitizing can reduce the risk of outliving your assets (what I ironically call longevity risk, as though living a long time represents a negative outcome somehow), but fees still remain a challenge.

47. "Yale CIO Disses Harvard." See also Swensen.

48. "Average Financial Advisor Fees in 2020–2021."

49. Geddes, 2019. Data assume no liquidation at the end of the holding period, implying a charitable donation or assets passing through an estate. With liquidation, the tax drag is not as harmful, but still a major negative impact of after-tax returns.

50. Ptak.

51. Swedroe, 2018. See also Ptak.

52. Securities and Exchange Commission.

53. Geddes, 2012.

Bibliography

Andonov, Aleksandar, Rob Bauer, and Martijn Cremers.
"Can Large Pension Funds Beat the Market? Asset
Allocation, Market Timing, Security Selection, and
the Limits of Liquidity." SSRN. Last revised November
15, 2012. https://papers.ssrn.com/sol3/papers.
cfm?abstract_id=1885536.

Ariely, Dan. *Predictably Irrational.* New York: Harper
Perennial. 2010.

"Average Financial Advisor Fees in 2020–2021." AdvisoryHQ.
https://www.advisoryhq.com/articles/financial-
advisor-fees-wealth-managers-planners-and-fee-only-
advisors/.

"A Winning Strategy." website of Ennis Knupp. White paper. 2000. *(Ennis Knupp is a former consulting firm. This source is no longer available to the public.)*

Barber, Brad M., and Terrance Odean. "Boys Will Be Boys: Gender, Overconfidence and Common Stock Investment." *Quarterly Journal of Economics* 116, no. 1 (February 2001): 261–292. https://faculty.haas.berkeley.edu/odean/papers/gender/boyswillbeboys.pdf.

Blake, David, Bruce N. Lehmann, and Allan Timmermann. "Asset Allocation Dynamics and Pension Fund Performance." *Journal of Business* 72, no. 4 (October 1999): 429–461. https://www.jstor.org/stable/10.1086/209623?seq=1#metadata_info_tab_contents.

Buffett, Warren. Letter to Shareholders. Berkshire Hathaway. https://www.berkshirehathaway.com/letters/1987.html.

Carhart, Mark M. "On Persistence in Mutual Fund Performance." *Journal of Finance* LII, no. 1 (March 1997): 57–82.

Cheng, Chu Xin. "Confirmation Bias in Investments." *International Journal of Economics and Finance* 11, no. 2 (2018): 50–55.

Clare, Andrew, Niall O'Sullivan, Meadhbh Sherman, and
Steve Thomas. "Multi-Asset Class Mutual Funds: Can
They Time the Market? Evidence from the US, UK
and Canada." *Research in International Business and
Finance* 36 (January 2016): 212–221. https://papers.
ssrn.com/sol3/papers.cfm?abstract_id=2589043.

Coleman, Murray. "Market Timing: More Evidence Why It
Doesn't Work." Index Fund Advisors. Updated May
10, 2021. https://www.ifa.com/articles/market-timing_
more_evidence_really_doesnt_work/.

Comer, George, Norris Larrymore, and Javier Rodriguez.
"Measuring the Value of Active Fund Management—
The Case of Hybrid Mutual Funds." *Managerial
Finance* 35, no. 1 (2009): 63–77. https://www.
researchgate.net/publication/228615633_
Measuring_the_value_of_active_fund_management/
link/55df8d7008aecb1a7cc1a397/download.

Commins, Patrick. "Economists Are Terrible at Predicting
Recessions." *Financial Review.* August 12, 2019. https://
www.afr.com/markets/equity-markets/economists-are-
terrible-at-predicting-recessions-20190812-p52g8r.

Dowie, Mark. "The Best Investment Advice You'll Never Get." *San Francisco Magazine.* December 2006.

Droms, William G., and David A. Walker. "Mutual Fund Investment Performance." *Quarterly Review of Economics and Finance* 36, no. 3 (Fall 1996): 347–363.

Duke, Annie. *Thinking in Bets.* Portfolio. 2019.

Ellis, Charles. *Winning the Loser's Game.* 8th ed. New York: McGraw Hill. 2021.

Elton, Edwin J., Martin J. Gruber, and Christopher R. Blake. "The Persistence of Risk-Adjusted Mutual Fund Performance." *Journal of Business* 69, no. 2 (1996): 133–157.

Ennis, Richard M. "Endowment Performance." *Richard M. Ennis* (blog). December 1, 2020. https://richardmennis. com/blog/endowment-performance.

Ennis, Richard M. "Institutional Investment Strategy and Manager Choice: A Critique." *Richard M. Ennis* (blog). May 18, 2020. https://richardmennis.com/blog/ institutional-investment-strategy.

Epictetus. *The Enchiridion.* Translated by Elizabeth Carter, 1758. MIT's Internet Classics Archive. http://classics. mit.edu/Epictetus/epicench.html.

Favaro, Antonio, ed. *The Works of Galileo Galilei, National Edition* (in Italian). Florence. 1890-1909. English translation as quoted in McArdle (2011). Original Latin version: https:// web.archive.org/web/20110718004557/ http://moro.imss.fi.it/lettura/LetturaWEB. DLL?MODO=PAGINA&VOLPAG=10-423.

Ferri, Rick. *Serious Money.* Self-published, 1999. https:// rickferri.com/wp-content/uploads/Serious-Money-Straight-Talk.pdf.

Festinger, Leon, Henry Riecken, and Stanley Schachter. *When Prophecy Fails: A Social and Psychological Study of a Modern Group That Predicted the Destruction of the World.* Harper-Torchbooks. 1956.

Galef, Julia. *The Scout Mindset.* Portfolio/Penguin. 2021.

Gazzaniga, Michael S. "Cerebral Specialization and Interhemispheric Communication: Does the Corpus Callosum Enable the Human Condition?" *Brain* 123, no. 7 (July 2000): 1293–1326. https://doi.org/10.1093/brain/123.7.1293.

Geddes, Patrick. "Measuring the Risk Impact of Social Screening." *Journal of Investment Consulting* 13, no. 1 (2012): 45–53.

Geddes, Patrick, Lisa R. Goldberg, and Stephen W. Bianchi. "What Would Yale Do If It Were Taxable?" *Financial Analysts Journal* 71, no. 4 (2015): 10–23.

Geddes, Patrick, and Robert Tymoczko. "Indexed ETFs vs. Indexed Separately Managed Accounts: A User's Guide." White paper. Aperio Group. 2019. https://www.aperiogroup.com/Resources/Papers/ETFs%20vs%20SMAs-A%20Users%20Guide.Paper.pdf.

Gilovich, Thomas. *How We Know What Isn't So: The Fallibility of Human Reason in Everyday Life.* New York: Free Press. 1993.

Gittelsohn, John. "End of Era: Passive Equity Funds Surpass Active in Epic Shift." Bloomberg. September 11, 2019. https://www.bloomberg.com/news/articles/2019-09-11/passive-u-s-equity-funds-eclipse-active-in-epic-industry-shift.

Goetzmann, William N., and Roger G. Ibbotson. "Do Winners Repeat?" *Journal of Portfolio Management* 20, no. 2 (Winter 1994): 9–18.

Graham, Benjamin. *The Intelligent Investor*, rev. ed. New York: Harper Business. 2006.

Grinblatt, Mark, and Sheridan Titman. "A Study of Monthly Mutual Fund Returns and Performance Evaluation Techniques." *Journal of Financial and Quantitative Analysis* 29, no. 3 (September 1994): 419–444.

Haidt, Jonathan. *The Happiness Hypothesis*. New York: Basic Books. 2006.

Haynes, Trevor. "Dopamine, Smartphones and You: A Battle for Your Time." *Science in the News* (blog). *Harvard University*. May 1, 2018. http://sitn.hms.harvard.edu/flash/2018/dopamine-smartphones-battle-time/.

Holmes, Millicent. "Improved Study Finds Index Management Usually Outperforms Active Management." *Journal of Financial Planning* 20, no. 1 (January 2007): 48–58.

Housel, Morgan. *The Psychology of Money*. Petersfield, GB: Harriman House. 2020.

Huston, Therese. "Hormones Can Make Men Mistakenly Overconfident." *Gulf News.* July 8, 2017. https://gulfnews.com/opinion/op-eds/hormones-can-make-men-mistakenly-overconfident-1.2054980.

Johnson, Ben, "Busting the Myth That Active Funds Do Better in Bear Markets." *Morningstar Commentary. Morningstar.* August 27, 2020. https://www.morningstar.com/articles/999669/busting-the-myth-that-active-funds-do-better-in-bear-markets.

Kahan, Dan M., Ellen Peters, Erica Dawson, and Paul Slovic. "Motivated Numeracy and Enlightened Self-Government." Public Law Working Paper No. 307. Yale Law School. *Behavioural Public Policy* 1 (September 8, 2013): 54–86.

Kahneman, Daniel. *Thinking, Fast and Slow.* New York: Farrar, Straus and Giroux. 2011.

Kahneman, Daniel, Olivier Sibony, and Cass R. Sunstein. *Noise.* New York: Little, Brown Spark. 2021.

Kang, Minjeong. "Do Hedge Funds Possess Timing and Selectivity Skill?" PhD diss., Arizona State University, May 2013. https://repository.asu.edu/attachments/110361/content/Kang_asu_0010E_12754.pdf.

Kinnel, Russel. "How Expense Ratios and Star Ratings Predict Success." *Morningstar Fund Spy* (blog). *Morningstar.* August 9, 2010. https://www.morningstar.com/articles/347327/how-expense-ratios-and-star-ratings-predict-success.

Krikorian, Martin. "Investment Fees You Don't Realize You're Paying." *Lowell Sun.* November 29, 2020. https://www.lowellsun.com/2020/11/29/investment-fees-you-dont-realize-youre-paying/.

Kumar, Satish, and Nisha Goyal. "Behavioural Biases in Investment Decision Making: A Systematic Literature Review." *Quantitative Research in Financial Markets* 7, no. 1 (February 2, 2015): 88–108.

Larimore, Taylor, Mel Lindauer, and Michael LeBoeuf. *The Bogleheads' Guide to Investing.* 2nd ed. Hoboken, NJ: Wiley. 2014.

Lewis, Michael. *The Undoing Project.* New York: Penguin Books. 2017.

Liu, Berlinda, and Gaurav Sinha. "SPIVA® US Scorecard." published by S&P Dow Jones Indices. Mid-Year 2020. SPIVA is a registered trademark of Standard & Poor's Financial Services LLC.

Madaan, Geetika, and Sanjeet Singh. "An Analysis of Behavioral Biases in Investment Decision-Making." *International Journal of Financial Research* 10, no. 4 (June 26, 2019): 55–67. https://doi.org/10.5430/ijfr.v10n4p55.

Malkiel, Burton G. "Returns from Investing in Equity Mutual Funds 1971 to 1991." *Journal of Finance* L, no. 2 (June 1995): 549–572.

McArdle, Megan. "Who Are History's Greatest Heretics?" *Atlantic.* June 23, 2011. https://www.theatlantic.com/personal/archive/2011/06/who-are-historys-greatest-heretics/240915/.

McCullough, Adam. "Do Tactical-Allocation Funds Deliver?" *Morningstar ETF Specialist* (blog). *Morningstar.* April 3, 2019. https://www.morningstar.com/articles/922123/do-tactical-allocation-funds-deliver.

Mooney, Chris. "Science Confirms: Politics Wrecks Your Ability to Do Math." *Mother Jones.* September 4, 2013. https://www.motherjones.com/politics/2013/09/new-study-politics-makes-you-innumerate/.

Morningstar Manager Research. "2019 US Fund Fee Study." June 2020.

Moser, Whet. "Apocalypse Oak Park." *Chicago Magazine*. May
      20, 2011. https://www.chicagomag.com/city-life/may-
      2011/dorothy-martin-the-chicagoan-who-predicted-
      the-end-of-the-world-and-inspired-the-theory-of-
      cognitive-dissonance/.

Nadler, Amos, Peiran Jiao, Cameron J. Johnson, Veronika
      Alexander, and Paul J. Zak. "The Bull of Wall
      Street: Experimental Analysis of Testosterone
      and Asset Trading." *Management Science*
      64, no. 9 (2018): 4032–4051. https://www.
      researchgate.net/deref/https%3A%2F%2Fdoi.
      org%2F10.1287%2Fmnsc.2017.2836.

Pace, Desmond, Jana Hili, and Simon Grima. "Active Versus
      Passive Investing: An Empirical Study on the US and
      European Mutual Funds and ETFs." *Contemporary
      Issues in Bank Financial Management* 97 (2016): 1–35.

Parkin, Simon. "Has Dopamine Got Us Hooked on Tech?"
      Guardian (US). March 4, 2018. https://www.
      theguardian.com/technology/2018/mar/04/has-
      dopamine-got-us-hooked-on-tech-facebook-apps-
      addiction.

Pompian, Michael. *Behavioral Finance and Wealth Management: How to Build Optimal Portfolios That Account for Investor Biases.* Hoboken, NJ: Wiley. 2008.

Ptak, Jeffrey. "Investing Taxable Money in Active Stock Funds? Bad Idea." *Morningstar Fund Spy* (blog). *Morningstar.* November 17, 2016. https://www.morningstar.com/articles/780229/investing-taxable-money-in-active-stock-funds-bad-idea.

"Putting a Value on Your Value: Quantifying Vanguard Advisor Alpha'." Vanguard. February 2019. https://advisors.vanguard.com/iwe/pdf/ISGQVAA.pdf.

Robbins, Christopher. "Behavioral Finance Helped Advisors Ferry Clients Across Coronavirus's Choppy Waters." Financial Advisor. September 8, 2020. https://www.fa-mag.com/news/behavioral-finance-helped-advisors-ferry-clients-across-coronavirus-s-choppy-waters-57859.html.

Rowley, James J. Jr., David J. Walker, and Sarinie Yating Ning. "The Case for Low-Cost Index-Fund Investing." Vanguard Research. April 2018.

Securities and Exchange Commission, Division of Examinations. "Risk Alert." April 9, 2021.

Segal, Julie. "History Made: US Passive AUM Matches Active for First Time." Institutional Investor. May 17, 2019. https://www.institutionalinvestor.com/article/b1fg0jnvbpc536/History-Made-U-S-Passive-AUM-Matches-Active-For-First-Time.

Shapiro, Fred R. "Who Wrote the Serenity Prayer?" *Yale Alumni Magazine.* July/August 2008. http://archive.yalealumnimagazine.com/issues/2008_07/serenity.html.

Sinclair, Upton. *I, Candidate for Governor: And How I Got Licked.* 1934.

Singh, Jyothi E., and H. N. Shivaprasad. "Behavioral Biases Affecting Investors' Investment Decision: A Review of Literature." SSRN. February 8, 2018. https://ssrn.com/abstract=3120503.

Smith, Emily Esfahani. "One Head, Two Brains." *Atlantic.* July 27, 2015. https://www.theatlantic.com/health/archive/2015/07/split-brain-research-sperry-gazzaniga/399290/.

Sommer, Jeff. "How Men's Overconfidence Hurts Them as Investors." *New York Times.* March 13, 2010. https://www.nytimes.com/2010/03/14/business/14mark.html.

Swedroe, Larry. "Is Alpha Enough to Cover Taxes?" Alpha Architect. December 26, 2018. https://alphaarchitect.com/2018/12/26/is-active-alpha-enough-to-cover-taxes/.

Swedroe, Larry. "The Names Are Never the Same." The Evidence-Based Investor. September 11, 2020. https://www.evidenceinvestor.com/tag/john-bogle/.

Swedroe, Larry. *Think, Act and Invest Like Warren Buffett.* New York: McGraw Hill. 2013.

Swensen, David. *Unconventional Success.* New York: Free Press. 2005.

Tetlock, Philip E., and Dan Gardner. *Superforecasting: The Art and Science of Prediction.* New York: Crown. 2016.

"Three-Quarters of Americans Are in the Dark When It Comes to 401(k) Fees." Businesswire. January 29, 2018. https://www.businesswire.com/news/home/20180129005124/en/Three-Quarters-Americans-Dark-401-Fees.

Thune, Kent. "Average Expense Ratios for Mutual Funds." The Balance. October 26, 2020. https://www.thebalance.com/average-expense-ratios-for-mutual-funds-2466612.

University of Birmingham. "Autonomy in the Workplace Has Positive Effects on Well-being and Job Satisfaction, Study Finds." *ScienceDaily.* April 24, 2017. www.sciencedaily.com/releases/2017/04/170424215501.htm.

Wright, Nicholas, D., Bahador Bahrami, Emily Johnson, Gina Di Malta, Geraint Rees, Christopher D. Frith, and Raymond J. Dolan. "Testosterone Disrupts Human Collaboration by Increasing Egocentric Choices." *Proceedings of the Royal Society B.* February 1, 2012. https://royalsocietypublishing.org/doi/10.1098/rspb.2011.2523.

Wright, Robert. *The Moral Animal.* New York: Pantheon. 1994.

"Yale CIO Disses Harvard." Institutional Investor. February 6, 2006. https://www.institutionalinvestor.com/article/b150npxc29brkk/yale-cio-disses-harvard.

About the Author

IN 1999, Patrick Geddes cofounded Aperio Group, an equity asset management firm that eventually grew to $42 billion in assets and a hundred employees by the end of 2020. Patrick served as Aperio's Chief Investment Officer from 1999 to 2014 and then as the firm's only CEO thereafter. Prior to starting Aperio, Patrick had been the first Research Director and then first CFO at Morningstar. Before Morningstar, he worked as a financial analyst at Amoco (now part of BP) where he learned the after-tax cash flow modeling techniques commonly used within corporations but rarely seen in the investment world (much to his bafflement given how much money it can save).

Patrick taught graduate-level portfolio theory and advanced corporate finance for many years at the University of

California, Berkeley, Extension. He has also had academic and practitioner articles published in the *Financial Analysts Journal,* the *Journal of Investment Management,* the *Journal of Investment Consulting,* and *Investments & Wealth Monitor.*

For more information about Patrick, including free useful tools for investors, news about upcoming courses, webinars, and more, visit patrickgeddes.co.

www.ingramcontent.com/pod-product-compliance
Lightning Source LLC
Chambersburg PA
CBHW051508150726

47997CB00001B/167